Emotionally Dumb
An Overview of Alexithymia

Jason Thompson

First published in 2009
by Soul Books

National Library of Australia Cataloguing-in-Publication-Data

Thompson, Jason. Emotionally Dumb: an overview of alexithymia

1st ed.
Bibliography
Includes index
ISBN 9781521957745 (paperback)

1. Emotional Intelligence. 2. Alexithymia. 3. Imagination

For Alice and Peter
whose voices will be heard

Contents

Introduction

To launch into a description of low emotional intelligence or 'alexithymia' is timely, for interest in the subject has grown dramatically since its original description in the early 1970s (Sifneos 1973). With the 1996 publication of Daniel Goleman's Emotional Intelligence came a further leap in popular understanding of the value of emotional skills for leading a fulfilling life, and conversely of the vicissitudes one may face without a good grasp on these skills.

Since Goleman's publication, emotional intelligence or 'EQ' has been studied in hundreds of thousands of individuals and results have provided a better understanding along with new methods for improving emotional capabilities. The initially separate constructs of alexithymia and emotional intelligence came to the attention of researchers who realized they were intimately related, with alexithymia representing the lower possible range of emotional intelligence. This realization has spawned a rich cross-fertilization of ideas, whereby aspects of each construct may be considered as opposite ends of a single emotional abilities spectrum.

Alexithymia is known to accompany a broad variety of medical and psychiatric illnesses, ranging from cancer or psychosomatic conditions to personality and posttraumatic stress disorders, touching the lives of thousands of sufferers and those in close relationships with them. The alexithymic person is unable to discriminate the usual nuances of emotional life, leading to immense difficulties in personal and interpersonal functioning. To feel and speak one's emotions seems a most basic human ability, so it is hard to imagine individuals incapable of recognizing and speaking about their most basic feelings. These difficulties are compounded by the lack of accessible (i.e. non-academic) texts on the subject. I hope therefore that the straightforward description of alexithymia in this book will increase general understanding of the condition. I further hope that an increase in understanding may help, both directly and indirectly, those most affected in coping with the condition.

In everyday language the terms 'feeling' and 'emotion' are often used inter-changeably. In this volume I will be using these terms in their more strict psychiatric sense where 'emotion' refers to physical arousal evidenced by such signs as smiling, crying, laughing, body tension, blushing, tight stomach, posturing, voice intonation, elevated pulse, etc., and where 'feeling' refers to one's mental recognition, understanding, and verbal accounting of the manifestations of emotional arousal. Alexithymic individuals may display full-blown emotions, but they do not necessarily understand the significance of these emotions on a mental level. To put it another way, alexithymia involves an essential deficit in one's ability to evaluate feelings, but not in the realm of emotional excitation.

Alexithymia may be to some degree a universal feature in all human beings, where we each display some anxiety, sadness or melancholia that is obvious to onlookers but not to ourselves; until someone points out 'You look a little anxious' and we suddenly realize we have been in the grip of a mood of which we had little awareness. Likewise we may not recognize when even our closest intimates show signs of irritation, anger or other emotion until they spell it out for us. Those with extreme alexithymia share this propensity but in a radical way; they rarely, if ever, have a clear sense of emotional states in themselves or others, and it is this pervasive deficit that researchers of the last few decades have sought to understand and define.

My interest in Archetypal Psychology combined with an intimate involvement with alexithymic individuals has fostered a keen interest in this subject, and led to the construction of an alexithymia questionnaire (see appendix) for those wanting an indication of their alexithymia level before undergoing the rigmarole of sourcing and financing a more thoroughgoing clinical assessment. In the following pages I will attempt to faithfully restate the findings of some of the main research on the subject to date, while comparing and contrasting alexithymia with a variety of subjects to provide a clearer picture of the condition. Throughout the book you will find a persistent mention of the stunted alexithymic imagination, particularly in the latter half of the book where I posit that these individuals may unlock their absent emotional understanding by gaining a better access to spontaneous imagination.

In chapters 9 and 10 include essays on 'Alexithymia and Metaphor' and 'Emotional Intelligence is Really Imaginal Intelligence' which were first published on Stephanie Pope's Mythopoetry.com website in 2008-2009, and have been updated for this volume.

Chapter 1

What Is Alexithymia?

Description

The behaviour now known as alexithymia was first described in detail by psychiatrists Peter E. Sifneos and John C. Nemiah, who were working at the Beth Israel Hospital with patients displaying psychosomatic disturbances. Many of these patients showed extreme difficulties in talking about their emotions, and in 1972 Sifneos coined the word alexithymia meaning 'without words for emotions' (from the Greek a = lack, lexis = word, thymos = emotion) to denote the cluster of behaviours he was witnessing (Sifneos 1973). Later that decade more researchers joined the emerging study of alexithymia, most notably psychoanalysts Joyce McDougall, Henry Krystal, and Graeme Taylor, whose 1997 co-authored book on alexithymia confirmed his reputation as a leading authority on the subject.

Over the past few decades the alexithymia concept has been refined theoretically, where it is presently defined by the following features:

1. difficulty identifying feelings and distinguishing between feelings and the bodily sensations of emotional arousal
2. difficulty describing feelings to other people
3. impaired imagination
4. thinking style bound to the external world
(Taylor, Bagby and Parker 1997).

Difficulty identifying and describing feelings

Individuals with alexithymia have difficulty recognizing emotional states as they are happening. They may on later reflection gain a vague sense that they were in the grip of a strong emotion, like tearful sadness or rageful anger, but are usually at a loss when trying to piece together what caused such emotions to manifest; that is, they cannot picture what stimulated the mood. At most they might have an uncomfortable sense of something changing inside their body – increased heart rate, blushing or butterflies in the stomach – and when pressed to give an account of their feelings, the alexithymic will have no words to offer, may fumble with a contrived answer or simply change the subject.

More often the individual will misread the physical expression of emotion as a physical expression of disease; for example, where the tears on the cheek become not sadness but a defective tear duct; the racing heart of passion, a faulty valve; or an anxious tightening in the stomach, appendicitis. One is reminded here of Jung's words, "The gods have become diseases; Zeus no longer rules Olympus but rather the solar plexus, and produces curious specimens for the doctor's consulting room." (1967, p.37) Alternatively, emotional states may be blamed on adverse environmental influences such as a change in the barometer, poisons in the air, or an uncomfortable mattress. It is as if there were a missing link that would allow imagination to form a picture of the emotional situation for the mind to work with. This then leads to the next point regarding the importance of imagination (and its lack) in articulating clear thought, for, as Aristotle said, 'The mind never thinks without a picture'.

Impaired imagination

Imagination is a complex phenomenon requiring definition before detailing its absence in alexithymic states. It is often understood as the ability to form pictures in the mind from the remembered stuff of our concrete sensory experiences. A closer evaluation of imagination shows it to be more complex, capable of creating novel images never before seen in the concrete world, yet still drawing on the bric-a-brac of scattered sensate memories to form its collages. Imagination can also present in ways other than quasi-pictorial images, where for instance one can imagine a smell, a sound or conversation, or a physical sensation on imaginary fingertips.

'Imagining' as I have described it here serves several important functions, such as our ability to imagine what our emotions, wishes, desires or needs are and how we would like to fulfill them; how we might imagine past and present-day conflicts; how we might regulate the type and intensity of our emotional expression; and how to imagine ourselves in another person's shoes, which latter lays the basis for empathy and the ability to be effective in dealing with the emotional states of others.

American philosopher Edward S. Casey (1976) has added a further layer to our understanding of imagination, namely the 'controlledness' or 'spontaneity' of any given act of imagining. Controlled imagining is characterized by a willful effort to manipulate images in the mind, such as when we deliberately 'use our imagination', whereas spontaneous imagining is strictly uncontrolled, unpredictable, involuntary and surprising. Casey shows how these two types of imagining are exclusive, meaning that imagination will be either spontaneous or controlled at any given moment and cannot be both at the same time, although in practice the two acts of imagining often appear in proximity and can give rise to each other in a symbiotic interplay.

To give a cinematic example from conventional science fiction, controlled imagination is the predominant mode portrayed by the lead characters of Star Trek, Dr. Spock and Captain Kirk, who visualize each course of action on their space odyssey in a deliberate fashion, leaving little need for a spontaneous dimension. In contrast Luke Skywalker of Star Wars takes a different approach by "letting go his conscious self" and allowing his imagination to suggest a spontaneous path. There are very different forms of 'imagination' at work in these two movies: one predominately controlled and the other spontaneous.

Whilst most literature on alexithymia does not discriminate which trait of imagining is in deficit, many alexithymic individuals do display a capacity for sophisticated controlled imagining, consciously using imagination for practical means such as how to work out a problem or construct a useful idea or object. This ability suggests that spontaneous imagining is the specific deficit in question. Several writers have noted this absence of spontaneity in alexithymic imagining, notably Fain and David (1963), Joyce McDougall (1985) and H. Krystal (1988). It is this second sense of imagining as spontaneous which carries the necessary experiential images of bodily emotions, and which is necessary for recognizing, thinking about, and verbalizing one's feelings.

For the alexithymic mind the intellectually controlled imagination is available, but spontaneous emotional imagination appears inoperable. By specializing in controlled imagining the individual does not have to deal with images which evoke sudden strong emotions; whereas in spontaneous imagination such emotions cannot be avoided and therefore threaten the individual's ability to cope. The deficit in spontaneity may point to a need to avoid such threats to the sense of self. (see 'Psychogenic alexithymia' in Chapter 2).

Thinking style bound to the external world

Without an ability to orient themselves within a recognizable world of feelings, alexithymic individuals are forced to orient themselves to the more limited physical world of external things. They are 'stimulus-bound' and 'externally oriented'. Indeed they are superadapted to the thing-world of sensate realities, material objects, and empirical facts, to which they apply their often impressive intellectual prowess. For this reason they are sometimes described as 'human robots' akin to the Tin Man from the Wizard of Oz who must chop his wood and think his thoughts without input from a human heart.

The alexithymic condition of 'stimulus bound' and 'externally oriented' comes very close to Carl Jung's early conception of the extraverted sensing type. As Jung puts it:

> No other human type can equal the extraverted sensation type in realism. His sense for objective facts is extraordinarily developed. His life is an accumulation of actual experiences of concrete objects, and the more pronounced his type, the less use does he make of his experience. In certain cases the events in his life hardly deserve the name 'experience' at all. What he experiences serves at most as a guide to fresh

sensations; anything new that comes within his range of interest is acquired by way of sensation and has to serve its ends. (Jung, 1971, p.52, first published 1921).

Jung's reference to experience refers to the imaginative elaborations of sensate activities, the ability to reflect on sensate happenings by way of subjective fantasy. He asks;

> What would the thing be worth if the psyche withheld from it the determining force of the sense-impression? What indeed is reality if it is not a reality in ourselves, an esse in anima? Living reality is the product neither of the actual, objective behaviour of things nor of the formulated idea exclusively, but rather a combination of both in the living psychical process, through esse in anima... the only expression I can use for this activity is fantasy. (Jung 1971, p.352)

A few decades after Jung, studies of this externally oriented cognitive style were brought into focus with the French publication of La Pensée Opératoire by Marty and M'Uzan (1963), who described utilitarian thinking and absence of fantasy in physically ill patients. The significance of these observations was further investigated by Nemiah and Sifneos (1970), who studied the cognitive style of psychosomatic patients. Their studies confirmed that many patients with psychosomatic diseases have a communication style characterized by a preoccupation with the minute details of external events and by an absence of fantasies. Around this time Henry Krystal (1968) was observing the same characteristics in post-traumatic stress disorder patients, whilst similar characteristics were being found in drug-addicted individuals, and those with personality and eating disorders. These findings have been replicated by numerous researchers to date.

Accompanying this external style of functioning may be a propensity to be guided rather by strict rules, regulations and social conformity which provide existential anchoring via their predictable codes of behaviour, rather than by feelings which for the alexithymic individual provide no such security. Children of, and those in close relationships with alexithymic individuals sometimes report the presence of moralism and pedantry, and may at times feel imprisoned by monotonous re-counting of chronological facts or mundane details of the daily round; all externalities which sure-up the predictabilities of the alexithymic world orientation.

Chapter 2

How Is
Alexithymia
Caused?

Biogenic alexithymia

Biogenic alexithymia results from physical abnormalities in brain
structure. These abnormalities may be caused by brain injury (e.g.
from a car accident), by lack of oxygen to the brain during birth, or
by the introduction of toxins. The abnormalities may also be genetic
or the brain may not develop properly from birth or during
childhood.

Researchers with a penchant for neurobiological explanations tend to
specialize in this area of thinking about the causes of alexithymia.
For example Sifneos, an early researcher on the subject felt that
alexithymia had a biological or developmental cause stemming
primarily from inborn predisposition, and several researchers who
followed stressed this view, and to be sure, there is proof that a
portion of these individuals have developed alexithymia
biogenically. It is therefore important for clinicians to ascertain
whether the condition is of psychological or biological origin, as
these causes may not be apparent in a superficial analysis.
Whichever cause is determined will have implications for the type of
therapy best suited to improving the individual's social and
psychological wellbeing. If neural structures are damaged and the
alexithymia is irreversible, then the focus of therapy should be on
learning new compensatory coping strategies as opposed to a
psychological education in feelings. While there is strong evidence
for biogenic cases of alexithymia, having had significant exposure to
members of the alexithymic community it is this author's

observation that such cases make up a minority of the alexithymic population.

Psychogenic alexithymia

It has been suggested that psychogenic alexithymia is caused variously by emotional trauma, developmental delay, or cultural and parental conditioning. Emotional trauma can be generated by experiences such as sexual abuse, neglect, witnessing or experiencing violence, being subject to physical pain associated with injuries, or chronic diseases such as cancer, heart disease, diabetes, and rheumatoid arthritis. Alexithymia is further associated with several psychiatric disorders (of which I shall say more later).

Trauma-rich states may elicit a radical blocking of emotional representations whereby images and symbols of emotion are aborted in the initial act of conception. French psychoanalyst Joyce McDougall states;

"[S]uch people had in fact experienced overwhelming emotion that threatened to attack their sense of integrity and identity… unable to repress the ideas linked to emotional pain and equally unable to project these feelings delusionally onto representations of other people, [they] simply ejected them from consciousness." (1989 p.95-96).

This absence leaves consciousness with too little data with which to identify emotions and convert them into speech. Primal repression is the theoretical term applied to this blocking activity (Krystal, 1988) a term which must be strictly differentiated from our more usual sense of repression termed repression proper. In the course of repression-proper, symbols of our experiences are allowed to form in the mind but are subsequently repressed from conscious awareness due to the unacceptable guilt or fear they induce. In the process of primal repression no such symbols are formed in the first place.

Primal repression is a factor common to a large proportion of high-scoring alexithymics, and in the words of two authorities on the subject J. Parker and G.J. Taylor, '[primal repression] may well account for the psychic structural defect and many of the clinical features associated with the alexithymia construct' (Taylor et al. 1997, p.89). This mechanism is further associated with communication idiosyncrasies whereby the alexithymic individual will attack perceptions which risk arousing emotional recognition – by falsifying, displacing, rejecting or omitting certain aspects of conversation in order to destroy those signals used to build emotional meanings. This also has the effect of obstructing personal links with the world and the people in it leaving all exchanges devitalised and devoid of emotional significance (Langs 1978). McDougall likewise concludes 'the continual effort to cut emotional links... to affectively charged fantasies and ideas, or to relationships with other people is a major psychic activity in alexithymic and psychosomatic states.' (McDougall 1985 p.170)

Primary and secondary alexithymia

The distinction of primary and secondary alexithymia was introduced in the mid-1970s (Nemiah, Freyberger and Sifneos 1976) to classify the permanence or transiency of the alexithymic state. Primary alexithymia refers to an enduring condition which seems to alter little over time or with changing circumstances. This form of alexithymia is not dependent on any temporary environmental or psychological situation. Its persistence is due to neurological defects or entrenched defences which may radically alter normal neuronal functions.

Secondary alexithymia has its genesis in reaction to emotional trauma, where the individual represses emotional representations as a temporary defence against further trauma. It is a state-dependent form of alexithymia, which disappears after the evoking stressful situation has changed. Stressful situations include various physiological or psychological illnesses, such as in severe depression or anxiety states, or environmentally maintained trauma or stresses. Secondary alexithymia is considered more likely than primary alexithymia to be responsive to therapy, although it is arguably still possible in the latter case.

Neurological structures thought to be involved

There are presently two alternative models of neurophysiological dysfunction proposed for alexithymia. First, the limbic-neocortical or vertical model proposes a faulty connection between the so-called thinking brain (neocortex) and the so-called emotional brain (limbic-system). In this model the emotional response centres of the limbic system do not share information in the usual way with the higher cognitive centres of the neocortex. When this neural pathway is dysfunctional the neocortex cannot access adequate information about emotional states (Nemiah, Sifneos & Apfel-Savits 1976). Second, the interhemispheric or horizontal model refers to the communication process between the two cerebral hemispheres, and the resultant pathology when this communication pathway is dysfunctional. Studies in 'split brain' patients –those who have had the large connecting nerve between hemispheres surgically severed to ease chronic epilepsy and other conditions– reveal an alexithymia-like paucity of fantasies, difficulty describing feelings, and an operative style of thinking. This has led to the hypothesis that functional interhemispheric noncommunication may be present in alexithymia in the absence of actual damage to neural structures (Hoppe and Bogen, 1977).

One could conjecture that in enduring cases of psychogenic alexithymia significant alterations in normal neuronal functioning might create atypical developments in the brain. If this were true, psychodynamic therapies might not be able to remedy the years of reinforced neural anomalies and accompanying alterations to brain tissue, serving as a reminder that psychological and neurological factors must always be considered together. However, if the neural pathways are still intact but underused due to the influence of psychological defences, there is a better prospect of minimizing the level of alexithymia by psychotherapeutic intervention.

As with the restrictively narrow neurobiological focus, it is important for those with a strong psychological view of alexithymia to bear in mind biogenic and neuropathic factors, to ensure the most appropriate therapeutic interventions.

Chapter 3

What Alexithymia
Is Not

Alexithymia is often misunderstood to consist in a lack of emotions, or a refusal to disclose one's feelings to others. It is neither of these, and in order to clear up the confusion we will here compare alexithymia with personalities which do evince a lack of emotional arousal or refusal to share feelings.

Psychopathy/sociopathy

Alexithymic and psychopathic individuals both can show a lack of empathy, insight and intro-spectiveness; are emotionally unresponsive; and may use superficial or contrived feeling narratives to facilitate social ties. But this is where the similarities end. These superficial similarities have tempted suggestions that alexithymia may be a cause of psychopathy, which is a serious error considering the number of opposing features presented by each condition. Alexithymics are typically socially conforming, ethically consistent, overcontrolled, submissive, anxious, and have difficulty identifying feelings, whereas psychopathic personalities are typically nonconforming, deceitful, ethically inconsistent, undercontrolled, dominating, anxiety-free, charming, and are often astute at interpreting and exploiting the feelings of others (Haviland, Sonne and Kowert 2004). Moreover, psychopaths have lower levels of emotional arousal than do alexithymics who may experience high levels of arousal but do not know how to interpret or respond to it.

Schizoid personality disorder

The most concise definition of the schizoid personality orientation is a fear of, and subsequent shunning of emotional intimacy. An individual with schizoid personality disorder (SPD) will go to great lengths to avoid emotional intimacy, and even though he is capable of emotional expression will suppress emotional arousal (sometimes to the point of extinguishing affect), leading to descriptions of such individuals having 'flattened emotions'. Their behaviour includes avoidance of interactive situations in which emotions may be stirred, or the person may participate socially while keeping their emotional life sequestered in a safe place in the self (Masterson and Klein 1995).

When emotional life becomes flattened or extinguished through various defences, schizoid individuals have little emotion-material available to feel, and will subsequently state that they have no feelings to report. This effort made to be self-contained and self-reliant also creates an interference in their desire to empathize with another person's experience; such an activity seems secondary, a luxury that has to await securing one's own defensive, safe position. This does not mean that a person with SPD has a deficit in their ability to interpret the meaning of emotional arousal; quite the contrary, they may be astute at recognizing the emotions expressed by themselves or others. In fact individuals with SPD may show skilled displays of communicating feelings but will almost never communicate feelings about themselves – the conversations in which feelings are aired almost always center on the topic of other people, social issues or issues tangential to their own lives.

In certain ways the operational mode of alexithymic communication has been compared with schizoid withdrawal, in that both seek to maintain a state of inner deadness to ward-off unwanted emotional experiences. While a lack of feelings and empathy are common to schizoid and alexithymic individuals, the underlying causes are very different: individuals with SPD decline to share their coherent personal feelings (when they have them), whilst alexithymics may show considerable emotion which they are unable to interpret and share.

Stoicism, and repression of emotions

Resistance of emotional impulses is best characterized by the stoic personality. Originally, the ancient Greek Stoics taught self-control and detachment from distracting emotions. By mastering the emotions they believed it possible to overcome the discord of the outside world and find peace within oneself. The word stoic is today applied to people who are unemotional, indifferent to pain, pleasure, grief or joy, those who 'endure patiently' in the face of adverse circumstances. The stoical person resists expression of their emotional impulses. On first sight stoicism may be confused with alexithymia due to the absence of communicated feelings, yet as in the example of the schizoid personality stoic individuals are not impaired in their ability to interpret emotion, rather, they have a chosen reluctance to entertain, act out, and discuss emotional matters. In fact stoic resisting of emotional impulses requires an ability to identify one's emotions in order to go about reducing their effects.

Different from the stoic's deliberate resistance to emotions is the emotionally repressive style. Repression functions to protect an individual from memories, impulses or ideas which would produce anxiety or guilt were they to become conscious. This further differs from stoic resistance in that not only does it keep certain mental contents from reaching awareness, but its very operations lie outside conscious awareness. When feelings are repressed in this way they may continue to find expression through a number of indirect neurotic symptoms, such as in nightmares or bodily symptoms which may superficially resemble the psychosomatic tendencies of the alexithymic. Nevertheless the emotionally repressive style (repression proper) implies the psychic production of representations and feelings which are relegated to unconsciousness, whereas in alexithymic states no such symbols or feelings are formed for a subsequent act of repression; they simply do not form, and there is no repressed material to 'uncover' in therapy.

Normative Male Alexithymia

A recent misuse of the alexithymia concept by Harvard University professor Dr. Ron Levant shows how easily the alexithymia construct can be misunderstood as a stoic resistance, repression, or denial of emotions. Levant devised the phrase "normative male alexithymia" to describe how North American males suffer to some degree from cultural conditioning which causes men to repress their vulnerable and caring emotions causing them to become underdeveloped in emotional expressiveness. He says, "Many men were raised (and continue to be raised) to function in a world that no longer exists. To be good men, they were told, they must become reliable providers, emotionally stoic, logical, solution oriented, and aggressive." (Levant 1997, p.3)

Levant further states the problem this way: "I believe that a mild form of alexithymia is very wide-spread among adult men and that it results from the male emotional socialization ordeal, which requires boys to restrict the expression of their vulnerable and caring emotions and to be emotionally stoic." (Levant & Pollack, 1995 p.239). Levant states that according to his clinical observation this type of problem is so common for men in our culture that it may be called "normative". He claims; "One of the most far-reaching consequences of male gender-role socialization is the high incidence among men of... the inability to identify and describe one's feelings." (Levant & Pollack, 1995 p.238) and "men are genuinely unaware of their emotions. Lacking this emotional awareness, when asked to identify their feelings, they tend to rely on their cognition to try to logically deduce how they should feel. They cannot do what is automatic for most women -simply sense inwardly, feel the feeling, and let the verbal description come to mind." (Levant & Pollack, 1995 p.239)

In light of these claims we must ask is it really true that men have an "inability to identify their feelings" or that males cannot sense inwardly and "feel feelings" as most women assumedly can? In one of only a few studies which found a higher prevalence of alexithymia amongst males, Salminen et.al, (1999) found that men assessed with the Toronto Alexithymia Scale (TAS-20) scored higher than women on factor 2 (difficulty in describing feelings), but there was absolutely no gender difference in factor 1 scores (difficulty in identifying feelings). This is an important finding in regards of alexithymia diagnostics because an inability to identify feelings constitutes the heart of the alexithymic deficit in emotional cognition, from which the secondary difficulty in describing feelings arises. If the difficulty in describing feelings does *not* result from the prior inability to identify feelings, but rather from repression or cultural proscription to "keep your feelings inside" then we are dealing with a different phenomenon altogether from alexithymia proper. Men may have the words, but they keep them inside.

While Levant may be right in his claim that men are generally less skilled than women in their ability to describe feelings, he is demonstrably incorrect in claiming that men are less able to identify specific feeling states in self or others in the true clinical sense of alexithymia. Here it would seem that Levant has failed to discriminate between the separate factors of (1) identifying and (2) describing feelings. The majority of alexithymia studies reveal that males are equally able to identify feelings in self and others, but occasional studies show that males are less able (or willing) to provide lengthy descriptions of the feelings they have successfully identified. What this means is that like women men can equally identify feelings such as jealousy, hatred, anxiety, fear, sadness, love, joy, envy and the like but they may not indulge a longer verbal description, preferring instead to thoughtfully act to modulate the intensity of emotions. This action empathy is in no way inferior to verbal empathy, and either of these responses typically employed by males or females can successfully modulate emotional arousal to desired levels: i.e. a woman might talk with her melancholic friend about what might be worrying her; the man may take the same melancholic friend to the cinema; both responses -talking, or acting-serve to intelligently modulate emotions.

To offer a recent research example which looked at differences in emotional intuition between genders, more than 15,000 people were assessed in an online experiment at the Edinburgh International Science Festival, led by Professor Richard Wiseman, of Hertfordshire University. Before undertaking the test each participant was asked to rate his or her intuitive prowess in reading feelings, with 77 per cent of women versus 58 per cent of men claiming they were 'highly' intuitive. Participants were then asked to observe a series of paired photographs, with each pair containing one genuine, and one fake smile. The results showed that male and female intuition was approximately equal, with men spotting 72 per cent of the genuine smiles and women detecting 71 per cent. What was more intriguing was that when it came to judging genuine and false expressions of happiness in the opposite sex, men were correct in 76 per cent of cases compared with only 67 per cent for women, a finding raising questions about the presumption of female intuition. Responding to these findings, psychologist Gladeana McMahon suggested that the reason women are labelled more intuitive is because they tend to talk more about their feelings, whereas men more often keep their intuitions to themselves (Fleming 2005).

In another study which did uncover gender differences in emotion recognition, Horgan and Smith (2006) discovered that different social expectations predispose males or females to be better at comprehending emotions in different contexts, even though their abilities in emotional recognition are equivalent. The participants in this study were asked to watch a video showing people interacting in different scenarios, and were asked for their views on what was going on based on the body language. Although they watched the same video footage, females scored better when they were told that they were being tested on their ability to make good social workers, but scored worse when told they were being tested to see whether they would make good interrogators. Conversely, males scored highly when told the test was to check their ability to become good interrogators, but poorly when told they were being tested for social-work skills. The results showed that when people were asked to play a role which was incongruent with stereotypical expectations of their gender, they performed worse. This evidence does not support the idea that women are better at understanding body language in every situation, rather that women or men perform better in selective scenarios because intuitive potential is subjugated to powerful gender expectations which encourage or discourage its expression in these situations. Therefore, both this study and the one by Professor Richard Wiseman indicate that there is essentially no difference in men's and women's ability to interpret emotional signals.

According to psychologist Mark Kiselica, past president of the American Psychological Association's Society for the Psychological Study of Men and Masculinity, most men are not alexithymic: 'It is not a norm.' In a speech given at the 2001 American Psychiatric Association Annual Convention Kiselica revealed that only a few studies have reported that males have slightly higher rates of developing the syndrome, while the overwhelming majority of studies found no differences between the genders, with overall about one in ten people of either gender showing any significant level of alexithymia.

True, men have not been educated or encouraged to express their feelings verbally but they most certainly can, generally speaking, identify both their own feelings and those of others as well as do women. From earliest childhood most cultures encourage males to be emotionally stoic, a disposition which may, as Levant stresses, lend itself to pathologies of emotional expression. But to emphasize the potential pathologies of this disposition tells us only a small negative part of the story. The stoic disposition also includes time honoured traits of forbearance, tolerance, and healthy emotional control in stressful situations. To champion emotional extroversion or cite verbal skill in expressing feelings does not guarantee healthy emotional interaction with others, as in the example of 'con-artists' or 'manipulators' who misuse the language of emotional expressiveness to exploit or domineer others.

To his credit, Levant has qualified his normative male alexithymia as a sub-diagnostic condition, which unlike true clinical alexithymia is not drastically pathological. Nevertheless, his conjectures reveal the twin errors of both genderizing alexithymia, and confusing it with general categories of stoicism and repression. In the final analysis this superficial conflation of alexithymia with 'maleness' may reflect the influences of contemporary gender stereotyping more than it does the findings of rigorous scientific method. It also leaves us with the unfortunate consequence of confusing the accepted clinical meaning of the term.

Shyness and social phobia

Shyness and social phobia are associated with the temperament of behavioural-inhibition, which is characterized by reduction in or prevention of a person's responses owing to the operation of some other mental process that 'gets in the way'. Unlike the repressive, stoic or schizoid personalities outlined above, shy and social phobic individuals often have the desire to express their feelings to others, which expression gets derailed by the unwanted incursion of anxiety. In a sense, the inhibition is created by an economic prioritisation of psychic energy – the anxiety-driven need to be cautious and the expression of feeling become incompatible, with cautiousness gaining the upper hand. The absence of demonstrated feeling here is not at root comparable to the inability to identify feelings in alexithymia – the shy and socially phobic individual knows what he feels.

Apathy

Apathy is a state of emotional indifference and unresponsiveness in the face of what would usually be considered highly emotive. Apathy is a common reaction to stress and is often associated with depression, but it can also be an aspect of temperament reflecting a non-pathological lack of interest in things emotional. Clinical apathy is considered to be at an elevated level, and the resultant passivity of feelings may be confused with the alexithymic inability to express feelings. Quite dissimilar too is the physical aspect of apathy, which includes lethargy and a loss bodily reactivity, which is not a feature of alexithymia; on the contrary, alexithymic individuals do show physiological arousal characteristic of emotions.

These examples show how alexithymia can look the same as other conditions in some respects, but must on closer inspection be differentiated from lack of conscience, fear of emotional intimacy, stoical resistance, simple repression, denial, inhibition, apathy and lethargy.

Chapter 4

Overlapping Concepts and Co-morbidities

In the previous chapter we looked at behaviours with extremely weak, if not false correlations with alexithymia. We will now take a look at the much stronger conceptual overlaps between alexithymia and autism disorders, obsessive-compulsiveness, posttraumatic stress disorder, and follow with a mention of some of the more common disorders and conditions with which alexithymia is correlated.

Autism and Asperger's syndrome

Ongoing research has revealed a significant overlap between alexithymia and autistic spectrum disorders (ASD). Two recent studies suggest that individuals with ASD exhibit a higher degree of alexithymia than matched control participants, with 85 per cent of the participants with ASD showing slight or severe alexithymic impairment (Hill, Berthoz and Frith 2004; Berthoz and Hill 2005). This raises the important question for future research regarding how to explain the high co-morbidity of alexithymia and ASD. From a clinical perspective the finding suggests that a diagnosis of ASD should be considered in patients with alexithymia.

This overlap has long been recognized on the higher, Asperger's end of the spectrum, which has similarities with alexithymic behaviour which have long been recognized. Every set of AS diagnostic criteria reflects the centrality of alexithymic characteristics: e.g. Lack of social or emotional reciprocity (DSM-IV); impaired or deviant response to other people's emotions (ICD-10); difficulty sensing feelings of others (Szatmari criteria); difficulties expressing themselves, especially when talking about emotions (National Autistic Society definition); emotionally inappropriate behaviour… impairment of comprehension (Gillberg criteria).

AS individuals have difficulty understanding their own and others' emotional arousal along with problems expressing feelings or reading the feelings of others. In AS there is also a limited imagination, an absence of symbolic thinking, and a pre- occupation with factual information. All these features correspond to the four defining features of alexithymia described in Chapter 1. The syndromes also share a propensity for psychosomatic disorders and hypochondria features (Fitzgerald and Molyneux 2004).

Similarities noted, there are features which clearly differentiate Asperger's syndrome from alexithymia, such as the tendency in AS toward stereotyped and repetitive behaviours (e.g. hand flapping). And while AS individuals are with few exceptions highly alexithymic, they may experience added difficulties in reading the objective, non-emotional intentions of others' minds. This mind-reading or 'theory of mind' (ToM) is the ability to understand and interpret the mindset of others, predicting their thoughts by placing oneself in their position and simulating their actions or beliefs. While some lack of ToM is thought to be associated with AS (Baron-Cohen et al. 1997), a recent study by Wastell and Taylor (2002) has indicated that this may not be a deficiency integral to alexithymia. It must be stressed, however, that studies of ToM in AS and alexithymia are only in their infancy, necessitating that initial findings be interpreted with caution.

Along with mild autistic behaviours and impaired ToM, alexithymia is one core factor of Asperger's syndrome as it is presently conceived. While this has not been strongly recognized in the past, it is becoming increasingly clear that the alexithymia construct is the most accurate, scientifically validated measure for gauging the emotional 'differences' inherent to Asperger's syndrome. As remarked by a leading AS researcher Tony Attwood, 'We now have a psychological term, alexithymia, to describe another characteristic associated with Asperger's syndrome, namely someone who has an impaired ability to identify and describe feeling states. Clinical experience and research have confirmed that alexithymia can be recognized in the profile of abilities of people with Asperger's syndrome.' (Attwood, 2006 p.130)

Obsessive-compulsiveness

The alexithymic individual displays mechanical, rigid and orderly behaviours, which according to two studies on alexithymia, has moderate associations with the trait of obsessive-compulsiveness (Keltikangas-Jarvinen 1990; Bach et al. 1994a). Alexithymics share most typical traits of obsessive-compulsiveness, including a preoccupation with orderliness and some degree of mental and interpersonal control; feelings of excessive doubt and caution; preoccupation with details, rules, order, organization or schedule; excessive conscientiousness, scrupulousness, and undue preoccupation with productivity to the exclusion of pleasure and interpersonal relationships; excessive pedantry and adherence to social conventions; a degree of rigidity and stubbornness; restricted expression of affection; inflexibility about matters of morality, ethics, or values; and excessive perseverance in behaviours or tasks.

These trait similarities apply to obsessive-compulsiveness, but it is important to note, however, that this overlap does not apply to the more comprehensive category of obsessive-compulsive disorder, a more severe condition which has a lower correlation with alexithymia (Zeitlin and McNally 1993).

Eating disorders

Eating disorders, such as anorexia and bulimia nervosa, are known to accompany disorders of affect regulation in which starving, eating and purging behaviours assist in regulating distressing emotions. As early as 1962 Hilde Bruch observed that these patients are often bewildered by their emotions and are unable to describe them. In Bruch's view therefore, attempts to provide insight were pointless as it entrenched the individual's difficulties in knowing what they themselves felt, and reinforced their belief that it has always been mother, and mother alone, who knew how they felt. Bruch therefore advocated a therapy aimed at increasing the patient's ability to identify and communicate their own feelings (Bruch 1962). This premise has been followed by later researchers who found that the primary deficit in eating disorders is the inability to process and self-regulate emotions.

To compensate for the deficiency in self-regulation, these individuals develop secondary pathological eating patterns to help modulate distressing emotions, which combined with the tendency to externally oriented thinking invites social ideas about ideal weight, which further reinforces the primitive self-regulation method.

Regarding bulimic behaviours, studies have shown that negative emotional states exist prior to binging, vomiting and purging, and that the majority of these individuals obtained emotional relief from anxiety or tension through these acts. However, the relief is usually short-lived, and a general worsening of emotional wellbeing is experienced through guilt, anger, shame and depression, creating a vicious cycle whereby the individual becomes trapped by their method of self-regulation.

The relationship of eating disorders with alexithymic traits is quite strong, with most studies showing around half of all those with bulimia and anorexia meeting the cut-off score for alexithymia. In one of the larger studies involving 114 females with eating disorders, 63 per cent of those with anorexia and 56 per cent of those with bulimia reached the cut-off score for alexithymia (Cochrane et al. 1993). The question of whether alexithymia in eating disorders is a secondary state reaction or primary personality trait cannot be answered definitively, as follow-up studies on those who have achieved an improvement in eating pathology reveal that most still reached the cut-off score for alexithymia, although a significant minority no longer did. Further studies are needed to confirm the stability of alexithymia in this patient group.

Posttraumatic stress disorder

Henry Krystal, a researcher who worked extensively with concentration camp survivors, has explored the links between posttraumatic stress disorder (PTSD) and alexithymia (Krystal, 1968, 1988). In addition to impairments in survivors' capacity to form imaginative symbols and in the ability to verbalize feelings, Krystal observed operative thinking, an inability to seek pleasure (anhedonia), and a lack of tolerance of emotional states – which all correspond to alexithymia. In PTSD the usual signalling function of emotion is lost, leaving no tell-tale emotion-symbols required for subsequent acts of interpreting, naming, and regulating of emotions. Instead, these individuals often go immediately from stimulus to response without psychologically processing the meaning of an event or providing a considered response. In contemporary literature the term emotional numbing is employed to refer to this emotional-processing deficit, which is considered a core defining feature of posttraumatic stress disorder. Emotional numbing is considered a more loosely defined analogue with alexithymia, and is characterized as the inability to feel both positive and negative emotions (Kashdan, Elhai & Frueh 2006; Litz et al. 2000).

Depending on the severity of the precipitating trauma and the severity of PTSD symptoms, the associated alexithymic traits will include difficulty identifying feelings and difficulty describing feelings in simple cases of PTSD, and in the more severe cases will further include constricted imaginal processes, and a stimulus-bound, externally oriented cognitive style (Sondergaard and Theorell 2004). This means that not all PTSD sufferers will display the entire subset of alexithymic traits, though they will all display some.

Personality disorders

To date, there is little data on the co-occurrence of alexithymia and personality disorders, though the difficulty of regulating emotions in some so-called 'primitive' personality disorders indicates the possible presence of alexithymic factors. In a 1994 study researchers looked at a group of 182 psychiatric patients suffering various psychiatric syndromes and found that 17 per cent of the sample scored in the higher alexithymic range, whereas 55 per cent did not (Bach et al. 1994b). This study confirmed a higher rate of alexithymia in schizotypal, dependent, and avoidant personalities, which emerged as significant predictors of alexithymia, but found only minor or negative associations with the remaining personality disorders.

According to James Grotstein (1986), borderline personality disorder may also be added to this list as alexithymia appears to be one of its conspicuous features, a position confirmed by several later researchers who cite the severe dysregulation of emotion characteristic of this disorder. Included in the borderline behavioural profile is the tendency to self-mutilate (e.g. by cutting or burning limbs) which supplies a primitive means of regulating and redirecting intense emotional states.

At present, more studies are needed on this subject before making detailed statements about the prevalence or relationship of personality disorders with alexithymia.

Depressive and anxiety disorders

Due to the difficulties involved in identifying and modulating the flow of emotions, alexithymic individuals may suffer significantly higher levels of anxiety and depression than do non-alexithymic individuals. Older studies on the relation of depression and anxiety with alexithymia yielded significant correlations, with typically around 40–50 per cent of individuals suffering anxiety or depression scoring highly on alexithymia measures, though it was not then certain whether the affective states fostered the alexithymia or vice-versa, or indeed whether this correlation remained stable over time.

 More recently a follow-up study on 137 psychiatric patients suffering major depressive disorder (MDD) has answered the latter of these questions (Honkalampi et al. 2001). In this Finnish study 45 per cent of those with MDD reached the cut-off score for high alexithymia, though on follow-up 12 months later only 22 per cent of them reached the basic qualifying line for alexithymia. Interestingly, the study found that almost all patients who had recovered from depression had also recovered from alexithymia, a finding which suggests that alexithymia may be largely a state-dependent feature in depressed individuals. As yet a comparable follow-up study on anxiety disorder is still to be carried out in order to pinpoint the relevance of state and trait alexithymia in this group. Nevertheless it is already clear from a multitude of clinical studies that alexithymia is strongly associated with anxiety and depression, no doubt aggravated by the difficulties these individuals experience in recognizing and modulating disturbing emotional states.

Clinicians would do well to bear this vulnerability in mind, as the alexithymic individual may be unable to articulate their very real emotional distress and ask for assistance. For the intuitive clinician the physical signs of anxiety and depression can be detected and steps may be taken to alleviate the symptoms.

Psychosomatic disorders

A psychosomatic disorder is one in which the physical symptoms are caused or exacerbated by psychological factors, as is sometimes the case with headaches, lower back pain, irritable bowel syndrome, asthma, nausea, allergy, hypertension or fibromyalgia. Currently, research indicates that individuals with a high degree of alexithymia may not be able to cope with life stresses by controlling their emotional states through mourning, self-soothing, sublimation, modulation, and other self-regulation methods. The hopelessness felt by the individual who cannot process distressing states is thought to initiate autonomic, endocrinologic and immunologic changes which incite psychosomatic illnesses like those mentioned above. This is not to suggest that all those with psychosomatic conditions are alexithymic, or that all those with alexithymia develop psycho-somatic illnesses. Rather, alexithymia is conceptualized as increasing a person's susceptibility to psychosomatic disorders (Weiner and Fawzy 1989).

Substance abuse

The basic problem faced by the drug-dependent individual is the inability to acknowledge their emotional needs and to exercise the self-comforting and self-soothing powers within themselves. They cannot do the kinds of things which ordinary people do to soothe themselves and relax, to channel distressing emotional states by 'treating themselves well'. This is one reason why the addict enjoys the drug-induced state, as it provides temporary relief from otherwise distressing emotional states. There usually ends up a vicious cycle, however, in which the calming effects of the drug intoxication are short-lived and the come-down only serves to increase the emotional stresses which elicited the desire for chemical relief in the beginning.

Several studies have sought to gauge the co-morbidity of substance abuse disorders and alexithymia, of which I will mention three representative findings. In 1998 Polish researchers investigated a sample of 100 inpatients with alcohol dependence and found that 78 per cent of this sample were alexithymic (Rybakowski et al. 1998). In Canada, in a group of 44 male abusers of drugs, alcohol or both, exactly 50 per cent were found to be alexithymic (Taylor et.al. 1990). In the United States a similar study of over 200 male and female substance abusers found that 41.7 per cent were alexithymic (Haviland et al. 1994).

There are still questions to be answered regarding whether the high incidence of alexithymia amongst is present before entry into drug dependence, or whether drug abuse itself has stimulated the loss of ability to regulate emotions. In the Canadian study mentioned above (Taylor et al. 1990) it was not determined whether alexithymia was the antecedent and the predisposing risk factor, a conclusion which could be evaluated only by longitudinal studies that start before people develop substance use disorders. Future studies may throw light on this issue.

Physical diseases and injuries

Diseases or injuries that are predominately physical in origin may cause an individual to develop secondary alexithymic reactions as a defense against pain. The experiences of radical surgery, accident or organ malfunction may unleash unbearable emotional forces which overwhelm the individual's ability to cope, leaving emotional flooding and unregulated affective chaos to be checked only through the deployment of primitive defences. In particular, primal repression may be activated to block imaginal-symbolic signals of affect from reaching consciousness.

This secondary alexithymic reaction is enlarged by a proposition from Graeme Taylor who posits a theoretical model of temperamental and alexithymic factors which predispose the individual to contracting disease in the first place. Taylor's model is based partly on studies by other researchers of cancer, heart disease, diabetes and rheumatoid arthritis patients which indicate that deficient emotional processing involves neural mechanisms that create dysregulation in the biological system, and which may facilitate the emergence of disease (Taylor et al. 1997).

Chapter 5

Associated Characteristics and Behaviours

Communication style

The alexithymic communication style is object-tied and logical, with a striking absence of poetic undertone which might reveal deeper resonances of psychic life. The alexithymic individual's choice of language is used to seal off access to inner mental life and to prevent the formation of meaningful emotional connections between their internal world and other people (Langs 1978). Said differently, the apparent efforts at communication are actually designed to draw another's attention away from interior experience and onto externalities such as the cost of food, the weather, or the person's latest forays into cooking, gardening, decorating the house, or studying architecture, i.e. there is a striking avoidance of any personal and meaningful self-disclosure of feelings, even when invited to do so. Discourse often amounts to long-winded recitals of facts and physical accomplishments such as 'where I went shopping today', not infrequently with little sense of direction or plot. For the listener such communication may prove frustrating, but it is essential to remember that the alexithymic individual has difficulties in expressing themselves emotionally and thus is attempting to remove all emotive speech from conversation. Such communication strategy is not motivated by ill intentions but by a sincere struggle these individuals face in defending themselves from interactions they find bewildering.

Many alexithymics learn to use common feeling expressions when they are being observed by others in order to compensate for their deficit. These take the form of 'potted-responses', such as 'My goodness!', 'Oh, that's no good is it', 'Wow! That's great', 'Gosh!' or 'That must make you feel bad', which form a small repertoire to be used in a variety of feeling-toned situations. With the right intonation, these responses can prove extremely versatile, covering the territory which for the non-alexithymic individual entails a more extensive vocabulary of hundreds of feeling-words and phrases. When asked, for example, 'Tell me how you feel, from the heart', most alexithymics can only answer based on intellectually constructed principles, and if they can't do that, the answer is entirely random because the idea of 'just knowing' or of something 'feeling right' is quite alien to them. So like the colour-blind individual who learns to cover up the deficiency with intellectual compensations, the alexithymic individual learns to inject a feeling tone into discussions, but using words which, unbeknown to the listener, feel artificial or insincere to the speaker who is 'acting' the part. These individuals may feel comfortable and even skilled at discussing intellectual subjects, but should feelings-based communication be called for then a repertoire of potted responses can helpfully cover embarrassing silences.

Another communication style (associated with less severe alexithymia) involves using speech which stimulates other people to act as vicarious regulators of their unprocessed emotions (Langs 1978). As alexithymic individuals have little recognition of their own thoughts and fantasies to assist in regulating emotional experiences, they have the tendency of ejecting these parts of psychic life in such provocative language displays that people they are involved with feel compelled to contain and reflect it back in a more digested form. For example, the individual may be expressing severe agitation in his/her body language and tone of voice in the company of a friend, and may continue with this display for hours until the friend becomes so disturbed by it that they offer up an interpretation of what the alexithymic person might be feeling, and why. Joyce McDougall (1985) refers to this behaviour as 'primitive communication' likened to an infant's cries or gestures intended to affect other human beings, who in turn respond like a mother who is moved to interpret and attend to a child's needs. It must be stressed, however, that the alexithymic individual instigates this interaction as the only way he or she knows to interact with others. The alexithymic individual may find himself co-opting the vicariously produced expressions of others, reminding one of a kind of reciprocal emotional mimicry not unlike that seen between a mother and infant.

Anhedonia and negativity

'No' seems to be the favourite default response of the alexithymic person. Even when asked a positive question like 'The weather is fine, would you like to go for a walk?', it is not unusual for an alexithymic individual to respond with a negative: 'No… well I'm not sure… do you think it's going to rain?', even if trying to affirm their willingness to participate. This nay-saying includes the tendency to point out what is wrong before considering what is right, including a preference for veto-power over assent in social situations, all of which stands as a negation of spontaneous self-experience. Sigmund Freud, we will remember, suggested that negation is repression: 'A negative judgment is the intellectual substitution for repression.' (Freud 1925, p.369)

This tendency to negativity has its roots in the need to prevent positive experiences from disturbing the otherwise controlled cognitive style, and is linked to the condition of anhedonia: the inability to experience pleasure from normally pleasurable life events such as eating, exercise, social and sexual interactions. According to Krystal the presence of anhedonia in an alexithymic individual indicates that the whole problem is of traumatic origin, with the individual retaining a sense of 'not deserving anything better' felt at the point of trauma. Those with trauma-based alexithymia have strong guilt feelings about experiencing any pleasure or gratification and tend to employ blocking mechanisms against consciously experiencing playful and pleasurable emotions. The general attitude, says Krystal, becomes one 'of suppressing and minimizing all achievements and maximizing the negatives.' (1988, p.253)

For alexithymic individuals this can become an area of fruitful exploration where practice in detecting the positive possibilities posed by others, and responding in the affirmative, can enhance one's relationships. While noting the negatives may be a valid way of assessing the values of any situation, noting positives has the advantage of affirming another's attempts to forge emotional bonds via joint agreement.

Hypochondria

Hypochondria or 'health-anxiety' poses the belief that one is suffering from a serious illness, characterized by irrational fears of being diseased or obsessions over minor bodily symptoms or imperfections. Commonly included is disbelief or doubt about the accuracy of doctors' diagnoses, combined with obsessive self-examination and self-diagnosis, and a preoccupation with one's body.

A typical alexithymic shows all the usual bodily signs of emotional arousal; racing heart, butterflies in the stomach, teary eyes and the rest. But there is an inability to identify these signs as emotions, and the individual is left to interpret the bodily changes as physical disease or illness: the anxious tummy becomes an ulcer or food poisoning; the nervous bowel, cancer or worms; and the amorous heart, arrhythmia.

It is worth noting, however, that the hypochondria associated with alexithymia is in no way related to the 'factitious disorders' such as Munchausen syndrome in which an individual intentionally fakes, exaggerates or induces mental or physical illnesses in order to assume the role of a 'patient'.

Sleep disturbances and poverty of dreams

Alexithymia seems to be related to poor sleep quality, in which the restorative process does not operate properly, with some alexithymics presenting as fatigued and unrested even after longer than average sleep periods. In a study by Bazydlo, Lumley and Roehrs (2001) individuals with higher levels of alexithymia were found to have dysfunctional sleep patterns – with decreased time spent in the deepest stage of sleep, and a parallel increase in the amount of time spent in the lightest stage of sleep (stage 1). The implication of this finding is that the increase in stage-1 sleep may contribute to a sense of having slept poorly and of general restlessness, whilst lack of deep sleep in stages 3 and 4 is responsible for a feeling of physical and mental fatigue in waking hours. The researchers also found a trend for those more alexithymic individuals to fall asleep faster than normal, possibly as a result of extreme tiredness.

In an interesting case of sleep deprivation and projective identification, I was provided an account by an alexithymic woman who felt her children always seemed tired, which was causing her concern. This woman herself looked sleep deprived, with general signs of fatigue and darkness around her lower eyelids, even though she reported having approximately nine hours of sleep nightly. On meeting her children it became clear that they were not suffering fatigue or tiredness and it was clear that the mother was projecting her distress about her own exhaustion onto the children. The children tolerated her concerns as another of her typical eccentricities and put themselves to bed at sundown, only to wake before sunrise each morning fully rested.

In the Bazydlo et al. study, above, it was suggested that rapidly cycling light sleep may account for the poverty and shortness of recalled dreams, though more research is needed before conclusions are drawn. In any case, most researchers report that alexithymic dreaming cycles are short in duration, void of stated emotional content, and 'banal', though there are accounts of highly disturbing dreams in cases of posttraumatic alexithymia. Much of this data comes from alexithymics self-reporting of what Krystal (1988) calls 'simple one sentence dreams' which are recounted in terms of concrete facts rather than spontaneous imaginal re-telling, which may well account for the poverty of affective resonance.

There are two further conjectures which explain the poverty of reported dreams, the first being from McDougall who suggests a tendency to eliminate new experiences and ideas from the psyche due to their emotional charge - an act which leaves these 'potential' dream elements unavailable for further deployment in dreaming since they have been foreclosed. She concludes 'there is nothing left with which to make dreams' (McDougall 1985). A second conjecture from my own observations reveals a selective repression of the dream's affective overtones whereby the narration is structured into a prosaic, non-symbolic description of dream objects, much as one would describe concrete things in the sensate world: for example, 'I walked into the kitchen and picked up a glass and then drank from it, then put it down and nothing more happened'. In this case no distorted aspect of dream content is recounted.

In all likelihood it may be found that a combination of (a) dysfunctional sleep patterns, (b) lack of new material for dream construction, and (c) selective recounting of dreams may together account for the impoverished dream recitals offered by the alexithymic person.

Involuntary emotional expression

Some alexithymic individuals manifest sudden and unpredictable episodes of crying, laughing, aggression and other emotional displays which are out of proportion to the aggravating stimulus, or discordant with the specific event. When questioned regarding the reasons for the outburst, they are often unable to link the behaviour with any memories or provocations, and may manufacture an excuse. For example, a mature-aged alexithymic man would sometimes burst into uncontrollable laughter when somebody was upset or had physically hurt themselves, including once when I had dropped a heavy case on my foot and was clearly in pain. On this occasion I questioned him about this response, to which he replied, 'I always laugh when somebody hurts themselves, because I'm nervous.' Others working with alexithymics have reported crying or sudden flashes of aggression in which the individual had lashed out or broken something in a rage. In these situations the usual defences break down, revealing a chaotic disarrangement in emotional responses.

A notable cause for such outbursts includes the operation of displacement, whereby strong emotions elicited by a previous stimulus are discharged on a new unrelated person or object. When faced with aggravations such as a financial difficulty, child frustrations or social stresses, the person is unable to recognize the emotional states incited by these situations, leaving them prone to sudden outbursts that are misdirected and displaced, sometimes under a slight provocation, onto the nearest bystander with verbal or physical demonstrations.

Intimate relationships

Intimate relationships entered into by those with alexithymia are often relationships of mutual dependency, and poor emotional communication can put a strain on them. Research has identified the alexithymic pattern of relating as corresponding primarily to the ambivalent attachment style, characterized by clingy symbiotic dependency, and secondarily to the avoidant attachment style, in which the person feels compelled to avoid contact with others. (Taylor et al. 1997) Although they form dependent relationships people with alexithymia may swap their dependency from one person to another with greater ease than non-alexithymic dependants, who typically become extremely distressed at the loss of a chosen attachment figure. People can become highly interchangeable to the alexithymic individual, who cannot easily identify emotional significance in others. According to Krystal (1988), when they do stay with one person long-term it is 'because they think it would be too much trouble to find another one, there being no difference between objects' (p.247).

Sexual intimacy may be another area of relationship difficulty, due to the poverty of spontaneous imagination and erotic speech, combined further with the lack of emotional significance of the act. Sexual relations may amount to a 'going through the motions' when there is little significance or meaning attached, but merely discomfort and confusion. Several alexithymics have reported being unable to cope with the bodily sensations of emotion when sexual activity begins to heat up, with some feeling violently ill with the associated affects. After many bungled attempts at relating sexually, there may come a sense that one is incompetent and that the whole exercise is not worth the effort or, as one alexithymic man noted, 'sex as a recreational activity seems kinda pointless'.

Perhaps the most taxing of relationship hurdles to be faced is of how to forge a relationship in the absence of empathetic attunement. Empathy is defined as the cognitive awareness and understanding of the emotions of another person, the ability to imagine oneself in the other's shoes and to respond appropriately (Moriguchi et al. 2006). For reasons already covered, alexithymic individuals cannot imagine themselves in another's shoes, and are therefore unable to mirror or help modulate the emotional states of others.

Although lack of empathy can place a significant strain on intimate relationships, that is not to say that a relationship cannot succeed without it. Indeed it is an area that the alexithymic partner can take steps to improve on and possibly overcome (see Chapter 7 'Therapy and Self-help').

Alexithymia in old age

Little research has been done to determine the relative increase or decrease in the level of alexithymia in ageing populations, though according to a Finnish study of a sample of 72-year-old people the prevalence of alexithymia was 34 per cent, a figure relatively higher than samples taken from the general population, which is about 10% per cent (Joukamaa et al. 2006). The precise reasons for this elevated figure are presently unknown.

Mature age comes with changes in cognitive and affective processes, which have an impact on those with alexithymia. Chief among these changes are the decline in memory and cognitive abilities, and the engagement in 'life review' activity involving increased reflection and reminiscence. Increased reflection may lead the older alexithymic to a recognition of their lifelong struggle with poor affect regulation and the enduring inability to seek pleasure. The accumulated losses sustained by not having experienced pleasure in social, sexual, relational, occupational and recreational spheres may strike particularly hard. There may also be, according to Krystal, a sense of uneasiness as to whether one is truly loved and cared about by other persons due to their inability to experience love or recognize another's affection for them. 'One has to feel love,' says Krystal, 'to be able to believe in its existence... [and] one has to feel love to be able to accept one's own self and one's own past' (Krystal 1988, p.241).

Chapter 6

Alexithymic
Parenting

Parenting is a difficult job for anyone and parent/child communications are often far from perfect. This is exacerbated for the alexithymic parent who may find it difficult to 'read' the signals and emotional cues given by their children. Fortunately, many of these communication difficulties can be alleviated by successful self-help techniques or with guidance from couples and family therapists with a working knowledge of alexithymia. In the following sections I will outline some of the more common issues facing children of alexithymic parents, with an emphasis on those parents who have not had the resources or opportunities to assess and improve their parenting skills.

Difficulty identifying feelings

Alexithymic parents typically cannot recognize, understand or give verbal accounting of emotional arousal in either themselves or others. Therefore they have a profound inability to recognize and help regulate their children's emotional life. For the child of an alexithymic parent this means that mirroring of his or her feelings and the ability to soothe, comfort and modulate distressing emotional states cannot be met by the parent, leading potentially to distress and repression of emotional expression by the child.

Children, particularly pre-verbal children, rely on parents to identify and help them to deal with their emotional states. This ability is relied upon by adults effectively to parent, and the majority of fathers and mothers inherently do 'know' the wishes and needs of their children, and successfully meet their needs. Clearly parents rely greatly on the presence of their own interpretive feeling skills; equally clearly, those parents who lack these abilities also lack crucial parenting skill. As Henry Krystal writes: 'Parents who have an exceedingly high rate of alexithymia are unable to assist their children in the process of affect maturation' (Krystal 1988, p.328).

Taking this lack of emotional awareness into account, one can see that parents with alexithymia have enormous problems conceptualising and understanding the nature and context of the feelings of their children. And to the degree that a parent lacks this ability and where that parent is the primary attachment figure, there is a risk that the child may develop anxious or avoidant attachment reactions to the lack of emotional support. If used repetitively over many years, such coping strategies by children may become habitual patterns of relating.

Misattunement and misinterpretation

Here we find the tendency to misread a child's gestures (e.g. child's crying, frustration or silence seen as 'bad' or 'naughty' behaviour) resulting in difficulties for children of alexithymic parents. As alexithymic parents cannot read their children's emotional signals accurately they may misinterpret the child's wishes, desires or intentions that conflict with their own as belligerence, which in turn invites misplaced interpretations, blame, criticism and sometimes inappropriate punishments. A three-year-old daughter of an alexithymic mother posed this dilemma to her father, who recounts: *I remember my daughter looking up at me and saying in her tragically innocent three-year-old voice 'Daddy, why does mummy always get it wrong?' She was deeply upset by her mother's tendency to deduce wrong conclusions or attribute incorrect meaning to her attempts at communicating... her mother could not properly read her face, her words, her gestures.*

The parent's inability to read a child's feeling-gestures and facial expressions (agnosia) may prove not only disappointing to the child, but may place them in danger in situations where, for instance, the child displays facial signs of pain or alarm and may need medical attention or protection from emotional dangers. When these signs go unnoticed the child's safety is jeopardized leaving them potentially exposed to psychological or physical harm. Moreover, there is a risk that if parents do not adequately assess the emotional suitability of other children or adults with whom the children are forced to keep company, the children may be placed at risk.

According to author of Emotional Intelligence, Daniel Goleman, by repeated successful attunements an infant begins to develop a sense that other people can and will share in his or her feelings, a sense that emerges at around eight months when infants begin to realize they are separate from others. This positive attunement is not experienced by all children, as may be the case regarding empathy deficiencies concurrent with alexithymic deficits in feeling. In a study reported by Goleman, Daniel Stern had mothers deliberately over- or underrespond to their infants rather than in an attuned way, and the infants responded with immediate dismay and distress. Goleman suggests that the emotional toll of misattunement is tremendous for the child, with consistent failures to empathize with the child's joy, tears or needs for physical comfort leaving the child prone to avoid expressing or even feeling emotions. If such misattunement is sustained the child may be discouraged from self expression and may lose large portions of the emotional repertoire necessary for intimate relations (Goleman 1996).

Random unregulated emotion discharging

As mentioned in the previous chapter, unregulated emotional expression may erupt in random outbursts, which are sometimes discharged onto the nearest bystander, and in the case of alexithymic parents the children may become the convenient target. The following provided by the husband of an alexithymic mother describes this behaviour:

> *Last night, the night before Easter, I purchased $100 worth of Easter eggs and planned to make it a joyful occasion for the kids. I noticed Anne was in an inexplicably tense mood, but not because of anything I or the children had caused, as far as we know. Anne suddenly burst out demanding the children do chores in a loud and intimidating voice, and then walked over to open a cupboard door in the kitchen (which I happened to be standing in front of) and proceeded to*

explode with another frightening yelling session at me for not getting out of the way of the cupboard quickly enough. The kids and I see this fairly regularly... I knew I couldn't reason with her, but as the children were looking frightened I decided to have a futile word with her pointing out that no one had done anything wrong, and that she was upsetting the children with her outbursts. Anne then started yelling at me for defending the kids (again who had done nothing wrong) and the children started to get panicky as they know this can get out of control when mom gets in her sudden 'moods'. After some 20 minutes in her tirade it then dawned on Anne, vaguely, that she has done something completely inappropriate, and so starts being sugary-nice to the kids. They of course respond back with a phoney 'nice' persona for mommy because they don't want to upset her, while feeling inside completely violated by her behaviour.

Often Anne will go into a verbal tirade against the children for seemingly no reason, or for some trivial reason. The children and I both know that if the child (I have two children) who is not the target of the tirade gets close to the fight, Anne will lash-out at them too, and so I advise whichever child is uninvolved to go and hide until it is over. This happens approximately twice every week to the children. After these outbursts Anne clearly feels better, as if she has gotten something off her chest, and seems almost unaware of what has just occurred, and then moves into a sugary caring mode with the children almost immediately. It's as if Anne feels apologetic, but at the same time is somewhat vague about what has just happened. After these events Anne rationalizes that the children simply must have been naughty, and leaves her thinking about the matter just there.

In such scenarios it is often difficult for family members to gauge whether the outbursts are related to present emotional events (i.e. Easter stresses) or whether some previous unrelated stimulus has fostered the outburst. Perhaps the most telling comment offered by Anne's husband was: 'I believe what really happened is that Anne didn't really know why she did it.' The outburst was an emotional reaction, but because Anne can't identify what is aggravating her, the reaction is likewise uncontrolled.

One explanation for such outbursts comes from Autism expert Tony Attwood who tells about a girl with Asperger's Syndrome who experienced difficulties at school and would later vent her frustration when she had returned home. He writes:

> 'Sometimes the anger is deliberately targeted at a person as a mood restorative. A girl with Asperger's syndrome was famous at school for her polite and compliant behaviour but notorious for the opposite when she returned home. She had contained her stress in the classroom and playground but on returning home was verbally and physically abusive to her younger sister. When I asked her why she was so mean to her sister when she came home from school, she looked at me as though the reason was obvious and replied, 'Because it makes me feel better' (Attwood 2006, p.246).

Support for the occurrence of random emotional discharges comes from several sources. Taylor et al. (1997, p.246-47), Joyce McDougall (1985) and Nemiah et al. (1976) each describe the brief affective outbursts of weeping or rage by alexithymic individuals, though it must be added that these outbursts are at odds with the usual descriptions of emotional control shown by the alexithymic person. According to anecdotal evidence there may be a relaxing of this emotionally controlled posture when the individual is away from the public eye, in private company. In public the individual makes a strenuous effort toward social conformity whereby energetic uprushes of affect are defensively held back; but when in private, the exhausting defensive armory may disintegrate allowing for emotional 'release'. This public/private dichotomy may explain why such behaviour has rarely been witnessed in public or clinical settings, whereas for children and family members who are privy to the contrast, the saying 'Angel in the street, devil at home' may bring an element of truth.

Exploitation of children's cognitive abilities

If parents with alexithymia require their children to self-identify, evaluate and self-regulate their own emotional states - e.g. parent asks child: 'Tell me why you are upset and tell me how I can fix it for you' – the parent may be placing premature pressure on the children's underdeveloped emotion-cognition and emotion-regulation abilities. Likewise, if a parent pressures the child to interpret the parents' emotional confusion the child is placed in the position of having his cognitive capacity exploited and overburdened. Object relations theorist D.W. Winnicott suggests that when placed in this situation the child has no choice but to substitute his or her mind in place of the maternal care and adaption which has not been forthcoming; the parent exploits the baby's or child's power to think things out and to collate and understand, and the child mothers himself or herself by means of this understanding. But such precocious intelligence in a child may be hiding a degree of deprivation in which there is held a secret desire to return to dependency and to be 'without mind' in the empathetic care of another (Winnicott, 1940, 1949).

Mechanical, externally oriented cognitive style

The alexithymic mother or father has a tendency toward externally oriented thinking in contrast to an interior or feelings-based thinking. The external orientation lends itself to a mechanical and sometimes rigid parenting behaviour similar to that of the obsessive-compulsive parenting style. Typical manifestations of this style may include a preoccupation with order, control and details; excessive doubt, negativity, cautiousness; conscientiousness, scrupulousness, productivity (to the exclusion of pleasure); excessive pedantry and adherence to social conventions; rigidity and stubbornness; restricted expression of affection; and inflexibility in matters of morality, ethics or values. These behaviours are extensions of the previously outlined 'stimulus-bound, externally oriented cognitive style,' along with the presence of anhedonia and negativistic subtraits.

Children of alexithymic parents may become experts in learning what they must not do, so as to avoid long-winded lectures, condemnation or punishment, but do not know so well what they can do as they have experienced mainly negative parental injunctions. Such children may feel that interactions with their parent are dehumanising, causing them to labour with each interaction. As worded by an observant alexithymic mother:

> *Just lately I have noticed that my children often do as their dad asks of them, but feel pressured to do the things I ask of them. The discrepancy is due to the cold hard orders that I dish out. Whereas their dad first creates a rapport between himself and the children (just a sentence or two), and then asks them to do whatever it is, I just see that something needs to be done and don't focus on the child, but the chore itself. I find it hard to remember that children are sensitive and need to be approached in such a way.*

Family relationships and support issues

In summarizing the preceding subheadings, these five characteristics of alexithymic parenting are considerable enough to promote disturbing and potentially enduring psychological problems for children. In the short term the child may experience anxiety, fear and feelings of insecurity due to the unempathic nature of the alexithymic environment. The cumulative nature of such experiences may establish personality disturbances, such as affective restriction, insecure attachment, communication difficulties, overdevelopment and reliance on the mind, and obsessional behaviour. Children of alexithymic parents are also more likely to be exposed to physical or emotional harm due to the alexithymic parent's inability to perceive emotional cues which would indicate environmental dangers or physical illness.

This chapter has limited its subject to highlighting the potential problems faced by children of alexithymic parents. It must be stressed that these children may achieve good-enough psychological health due to influences of non-alexithymic family members, parents (if one is present) and of the child's peers. As Henry Krystal notes, the fact some children 'resembled their peers more than their parents in the nature of their affect maturation, fantasy formation, and affect tolerance suggests that the social element and identification with peers during latency and adolescence may account for the demonstrated cultural variation in their affect differentiation' (Krystal 1988, p.328).

I would elaborate Krystal's statement further and say it is of vital importance that these children, particularly in their pre-adolescent phases of development, have extensive contact with all non-alexithymic support persons, and particularly with the non-alexithymic parent if one is available to provide empathy and support for the emotional development of the child. The non-alexithymic parent would certainly be more valuable than 'peers' in helping such children, because emotional development moves through crucial phases particularly in infancy and toddlerhood when peers are less available than parents who are caring for the child around the clock. Certainly, without non-alexithymic support persons the psychological future of the exclusively alexithymic-parented child may be a problematic one.

Support for the alexithymic family, where possible in the form of input from non-alexithymic intimates is an important consideration which I submit would be welcomed by those with the condition. Many individuals with alexithymia are aware that they possess a deficit in emotion-cognition largely due to the feedback they receive from others, and as a result of this awareness typically gravitate towards support persons who might help them interpret and navigate the world of emotional concerns. This amenability to receiving support was pointed out by one alexithymic mother who stated: 'I like the old phrase that "It takes a whole community to raise a child", because I can't do it on my own and find it a whole lot easier with help.'

Regarding adult individuals who were parented by an alexithymic parent or parents and who now experience difficulties in emotional expression, some words of hope come from author Daniel Goleman who describes the ability to continually reshape our models of relating as an ongoing process where imbalances experienced in childhood may be corrected later. He suggests that psychotherapy may help to provide just such an emotional corrective, based on the therapist's ability to be empathetically attuned, much like a good-enough mother is with her infant. 'The emotional synchrony', states Goleman of the therapeutic relationship, 'is unstated and outside conscious awareness, though a patient may bask in the sense of being deeply acknowledged and understood' (Goleman 1996, p.102).

Considering there has been over 30 years of research on alexithymia and its effects on communication it seems surprising that no one –to my knowledge- has looked closely at the problems faced by the 'alexithymic family'. This is also a matter of concern in regards to children who are in the sole care of such a parent after marital separation. Given the communication dysfunction alexithymic parents often face in their spousal relationships, it is plausible that many of these relationships would be placed under additional stress and break down due to emotional missattunement. If such breakdowns are indeed commonplace, it seems remarkable that concerns about alexithymia have not yet been seen in custody, access or child-welfare case law. Specifically, the issue here must firstly be to ask how much help and support is needed by an alexithymic parent to care for his/her children successfully.

According to a Swedish study, having a low level of social support was found to be 3.5 times more common in the alexithymic population and 2.6 times more common for these individuals not to have someone to turn to in stressful situations (Posse, Hallstrom and Backenroth-Ohsako 2002). Based on these indications it would be prudent for clinicians to consider the support needs of alexithymic individuals in personal, social and familial arenas, and if necessary to introduce them to child-welfare agencies, social workers, or counsellors who might help them to develop useful coping strategies in these areas.

Chapter 7

Therapy and Self-help

Biofeedback

Biofeedback is by definition a feeding back to conscious aware- ness of biological functions such as breathing, heart rate, skin temperature, muscle tension and other physiological manifestations of which the person is sometimes unaware. Many alexithymic individuals are aware that they react differently to other people, so when they are helped through biofeedback therapy to recognize their emotional responses and their usual inability to identify and classify them, they gain a sense of perspective and some relief in knowing they are not crazy. Emotion-naming requires time and patience to wait for the appearance of each emotion bodily before identifying characteristics and finding the terminological 'match', and the process must be repeated many times over before the ability to classify becomes fluent. Merely providing the individual with a compendium of feeling words in the absence of biofeedback proves of little value in the task of recognition. By learning to classify their emotions, alexithymic persons gain an intellectual sense of what is taking place bodily, and may for the first time consider these manifestations in terms other than physical illness.

However, such intellectual guesswork, while helpful in understanding some emotions, may still fall short of the specificity of imaginal feedback on emotional states (discussed in the next section). The strictly intellectual attempt at classifying sometimes finds discrimination between feelings difficult, for example:

> I find myself at an amusement park with a lover and notice my heart is racing, so I ask: 'Is my racing heart anxiety-based

due to my of fear being around crowds?… Is it because I'm excited about the ride we are lining up for?… Is it because I'm in love?… Is it because I feel amorous?… Is it because I'm angry about the guy who just pushed in the line in front of me?… Or is it because I forgot to take my blood pressure medication this morning?

This scenario presents six distinct choices, and it may be hard to tell which one is relevant based on circumstantial clues of the environment or by bodily signals alone. Imaginal feedback on the other hand shows the specific face of emotion, where my rapid heart rate appears together with an image of a tender couple standing in line, and I know that the beating is of a 'loving heart'.

Biofeedback therapies may include techniques which improve recognition of spontaneously produced emotion-symbols that go to help identify feelings, along with further techniques in controlled visualisation to aid regulation of emotions. But these objectives presuppose an ability to access and use imagination through introspection, which is difficult for alexithymic persons. While biofeedback therapies often include work with imaginal processes, for the sake of clarity we will treat these under a separate heading in order to differentiate imaginal representations from purely intellectual inferences about body sensations.

Imaginal feedback

Images can help us identify our emotions in any situation, as in the amusement park example above of becoming aware of one's beating heart (biofeedback) and subsequently intellectualising six possible events and resultant emotions that could be causing it. In this instance, the internal fantasy image, two lovers in an embrace, allows one to discriminate, to understand, to relate more deeply to the emotion being experienced. Images as spontaneous signifiers of emotion have the power to unlock the absent emotional understanding, and this fact may prove especially relevant for the alexithymic individual. But first we must acknowledge that fantasy images are not available to conscious awareness for the alexithymic individual, either because of damaged brain structures or psychological blocking defences. The aim of this discussion, then, is to offer a therapeutic avenue for creating greater access to these images.

In the case of psychogenic alexithymia, therapeutic work can be done to remove defensive blockages, allowing imaginal signifiers to reach consciousness and provide feedback on the emotional happenings of the body. Before detailing techniques used in imagination-focused therapy, it is first worth understanding some of the known psychodynamic issues likely to be con- fronted with these patients. Therapy with the alexithymic individual is bound up with object relations (internalised images of significant people – the mother, father, teacher, family member, spouse) which requires a deeper, more thoroughgoing analysis than a superficial education in biofeedback or imaginal techniques. For instance, Henry Krystal has found that these patients are very poor at taking care of themselves, are not conscious of their reluctance to do so and are uninterested in correcting it. This reluctance, relates Krystal, is based on a fear that the individual's vital functions including emoting, imagining, fantasying, self-caring and self-soothing, are the province of maternal objects forbidden to them for purposes of self-governance.

It is difficult for the alexithymic individual to let go of their reliance on a significant other as interpreter and governor of these functions. The formation and recognition of imaginal signs, plus their personal deployment in regulating emotion, is under the strictest taboo; they are 'powers', writes Krystal, 'reserved for mother, doctor, God'… but most certainly not for oneself (1988, p.317). The operation of this taboo explains the tendency for alexithymic individuals to project their feelings onto significant others (e.g. mother, doctor, friend, spouse, or indeed their own children), so that those feelings can be interpreted and reflected back in more digested form. Because this mimics an infant's emotional dependence on its mother, such significant others are known in psychodynamic theory as maternal transference objects.

It should be noted that a strong sense of resentment may be experienced towards maternal transference objects for, as the alexithymic individual comes to feel it, the significant other (interpreter) has usurped their power and is withholding permission for the individual to govern their own life. For example, if an alexthymic individual had their car stolen, they may have to offer this experience up to the significant other for emotional interpretation, and may then feel resentful for having lost the power to make sense of the experience for themselves. This puts the significant other in the peculiar position of being simultaneously encouraged to take control and despised for doing so. In therapy, this resentful transference reaction can prove useful for elaborating with the patient the sense of powerlessness they have experienced their whole life, and allows for further explorations about the value and possibilities of self-governance, though one must approach this subject with great care due to the operation of the taboo.

Without knowledge of the taboo the naïve therapist may be perplexed at the unwillingness of these patients to recognize, verbalize, or regulate their own emotions. To the alexithymic individual the therapist is asking something unthinkable and dangerous, and without proper understanding of these issues the therapist and the patient are likely to come to a stalemate. For the attuned therapist the pseudophobia (Krystal 1988) surrounding emotion and imagination must be relieved before further progress can be made in the area of self-control over these functions. This is a huge task, which also involves coming to terms with the experience of a lifetime of emotional deprivation and with an impaired capacity to develop loving relationships. This is akin to a grieving process. Moreover, the renewed ability to believe that love is real and that love works is essential before the products of imagination can be adequately accessed.

Entertaining the possibility that they might be able to self-govern their emotions and that their self governance might be allowed and even encouraged under the loving eye of another, is asking them to exercise their imagination in the most powerful way and, in the words of Krystal, 'it may be the most daring thing we invite patients to do– to participate with the analyst in exercising their imagination' (1988, p.332). If the grieving process is traversed and the patient is allowed to experience love through an open acceptance of their spontaneous imaginal gestures, they can then develop the ability to find imaginative ways of soothing themselves when in states of distress, and to self-regulate their emotions rather than relying on others (mother, therapist) to fulfill these tasks for them. The therapist must be prepared to facilitate this process slowly, subtly and patiently, at a pace that is set by the patient, in order to allow the patient to experience the possibility of self-control over this process.

A whole new field of psychology is opening up to the possibility of using imagination therapeutically. Whilst there are too many instances of 'image focused therapy' to treat in this short volume, it is perhaps worth mentioning the school of archetypal psychology, as elaborated by James Hillman (1983). Archetypal psychology has developed a sophisticated set of guidelines for evoking and vivifying the patient's imagination (that is, keeping it alive) in the therapeutic setting, a process having immediate value for enriching the impoverished imagination of alexithymic individuals. This method asks the imaginal therapist to be guided by questions such as: 'How well has the image worked? Does the image release and refine further imagining? Does the therapist's response "stick to the image" as the task at hand, rather than associate or amplify into non-imagistic symbolisms, personal opinions, and interpretations?' (Hillman, 1983, p.21). The therapist and patient must use these questions to guard against losing the emerging image through intellectual distractions.

These questions hold the therapist to the singular task of 'animating the image', because according to the premises of archetypal psychology the image is the primary psychological datum, in which feelings are as complex as the image that contains them. This approach necessitates that therapy *return personal feelings (anxiety, desire, confusion, boredom, misery) to the specific images which hold them. Therapy attempts to individualize the face of each emotion: the body of desire, the face of fear, the situation of despair. Feelings are imagined into their details.'* (Hillman 1983, p.59)

Archetypal psychology's techniques are essentially elaborations of the Jungian method of active imagining, consisting in the open contemplation of spontaneously produced images and fantasies, enabling a dialectical relation between an individual's emotional fantasies and the attentive ego. Once the ego has been enriched by this information, the individual is afforded necessary material with which to conclude a specific feeling valuation, including the ability to name one's own emotional experience with the appropriate words.

In conjunction with the increased ability to process spontaneous emotion-images through active imagining, the alexithymic patient may form nascent abilities of controlled imagining for the purpose of affect regulation; that is, they may learn to visualize their desired preferences to express, inhibit or sublimate a given emotional response. In other words, understanding the emotion may then offer the patient the ability to decide what to do with the energy that emotion has created. For example, if the person becomes angry and recognizes the force and source of the anger, they may be able to visualize how to respond in a creative way. Instead of having to find an external regulator, the patient may now have the choice to direct or redirect that emotional energy; that is, direct their anger at the person that has caused the upset or redirect it into another activity, a house-cleaning frenzy for example.

Such ability to manage emotions is the keystone to emotional intelligence, and if the alexithymic individual is able to improve his access to imaginal processing it is likely to show as a reduction in alexithymic traits and an improvement on emotional intelligence measures. While biofeedback is a very important tool in helping alexithymics understand their emotions, imaginal feedback offers the patient an opportunity to target the exact source of their feelings and offers them a chance at genuine self-expression. The axiom to be drawn here is that if imagination cannot be accessed, then neither can feelings be accessed.

Self-help

Intractable cases of alexithymia, particularly those with biogenic causes, may not lend themselves to imaginal feedback techniques. If the neural structures involved in emotion-processing are damaged by injury or atrophy, the process may not be reversible. Moreover, even for those with a treatable form of alexithymia, psychotherapy may be impractical due to travel constraints or extravagant costs. In these cases compensatory coping strategies are prescribed to help one function as well as possible in personal and public life. These strategies range from educative explorations to help clarify the nature of one's difficulties, to tailored practical 'self-help' strategies for better handling inter- personal relating and crises. Along these lines the following suggestions may be useful for those who have alexithymia:

Recognize alexithymia – don't ignore it
If you have heard about alexithymia and suspect you have it, take time to read more about the function or dysfunction of emotional awareness in everyday life, and try to identify corresponding aspects of your own experience. Most literature on emotional intelligence, and particularly titles about Asperger's syndrome, tend to cover this subject. This proactive approach will prove more beneficial than ignoring alexithymia, as it prepares the way for self-help techniques to be targeted to those areas in which you experience setbacks. In the long run the awareness gained will help your life to become more manageable, adjusted and enjoyable.

Accept yourself
During the discovery process you will learn that you do not have an inadequate personality, but that you are different in a beneficial way and possess valuable qualities as part of that difference. Some of the noted qualities alexithymic individuals display are loyalty, dependability, ability to speak one's mind, a skill for noticing detail, exceptional memory for certain facts (such as names, dates, schedules, routines), a desire for order and accuracy, an acute sensitivity to physical stimuli (hearing, touch, vision and/or smell), increased perseverance and endurance in areas of interest, and not infrequently a prowess in certain sports or games (Attwood and Gray 1999). These traits are valued, and even desired, by those who lack them, which knowledge can contribute to general self-acceptance as you evaluate both the weaknesses and strengths in your character.

Practice detecting emotions
Learn to familiarize yourself with the possible signs of emotion, such as a racing heart, feeling faint, blushing, breathlessness, body-tension, goose-bumps, butterflies, sickness or pain in the stomach. When such symptoms appear it will be difficult for you to distinguish whether these signs are from emotions or physical illnesses, such is the conundrum posed by alexithymia. But it is worth asking the question in order to save yourself unnecessary trips to the doctor due to misinterpretation of body states. You may be able to make a hypothetical connection between the physical signs

and current life-events or circumstances which might have elicited the reaction in your body.

If you have some vague sense that the symptoms may be emotional, try to find techniques whereby you can reduce the physical effects of these emotions in your body even if you can't quite identify which emotions they are. There are general ways to achieve this, such as by reducing the quantity of your activities, slowing down your pace, relaxing or lying down to rest, all of which may alleviate the upsetting effects of emotional stress. On these occasions it may help to do self-comforting activities like listening to soothing music or preparing a favourite meal.

A second technique is to selectively change your present circumstances – your schedule, your present projects, or even the company you keep with others – to see if this removes the evoking stressors. If this does remove the stressors, your body will feel less tense and any ill-feeling will dissipate.

Third, try injecting a new activity into your schedule and start it immediately, preferably an enjoyable one such as a favourite sport, hobby, watching TV or visiting a friend. This frequently succeeds in redirecting an uncomfortable emotional state, such as depression or sadness, replacing it with more enjoyable ones. There will of course be times when these methods don't work, but take heart – even non-alexithymic people can't always control their emotions.

Learn techniques in 'emotional etiquette'
Because you will be mixing with non-alexithymic people much of the time you will benefit by cultivating a keener sense of others' emotional messages judging by their verbal and physical cues, such as smiling and crying. If you have a vague idea of what the other person might be feeling – even if you can only detect such broad categories as 'good' and 'bad' or 'happy' and 'sad' – this will be a good basis on which to craft your response. If you can recognize these general categories of feeling, you can respond also with general 'potted responses' which pass as polite and acceptable exchanges, even if you don't understand the fuller complexity of others' feelings. These versatile responses can be (a) generalised comments of concern toward the other person's unhappiness (e.g.

'That's no good' or 'That must make you feel awful') or (b) a praising response toward others' sense of good fortune or happiness (e.g. 'Wow! You must be happy about that' or 'I'm really happy for you'). Such broad responses pass as acceptable emotional etiquette which do not require you to look for deeper emotional nuances.

A further useful technique in emotional etiquette, and one which enormously benefits those with alexithymia is the so-called 'compliment – critique - compliment' technique. Alexithymic individuals are noted for being direct with their stated opinions, which to a non-alexithymic person can seem deliberately rude or hostile.

Without clear qualifiers of the emotional intent behind your statement, non-alexithymic persons may suspect that kind words have been deliberately withheld from statements as an act of unfriendliness. To avoid this gross misunderstanding it pays to soften one's statements with a compliment before offering a blunt factual observation. For example, where an alexithymic individual might point out to a mathematics student 'Your answer to that equation is incorrect', a more reassuring approach might go something like '[compliment] I like the way you set out your work, I can see you've put a lot of effort into it… [critique] but on this occasion the answer to the equation is incorrect… [compliment] but good luck on the next question, I hope you do better'.

The encouraging statements offered here both before and after the factual critique qualifies the emotional tone and motivation of the speaker. If no qualification is offered, then the hearer may feel that the speaker is just being unfriendly. Learning to use qualifiers and simple feelings responses like those outlined above may feel somewhat automated or phoney, but they will nevertheless get you through to your old age with the least amount of heartache to yourself from misunderstandings, and for this reason they are worth employing.

Be wary of commonsense advice about feelings
Be wary of friends bearing commonsense advice about 'how to get in touch with your feelings'. Acquaintances who gain a sense of how difficult it is for you to apprehend your feelings may suggest body-

relaxation, meditation, self-esteem affirmations, expressive discussions, primal-screaming, and other random techniques. These suggestions are usually intended for people with proficiency in the normal range of feelings, and may not be suitable for alexithymics. In fact they may even lead to confusion, frustration and physical turmoil when your emotions become stirred and find you cannot modulate their effects.

Create a stable routine

Without the ability to self-regulate your emotions efficiently, it is very difficult to modulate the level of anxiety that comes with meeting new people or facing unfamiliar circumstances. There- fore some people with alexithymia find it helpful to maintain a stable predictable routine to help control the sheer quantity of new emotional information that has to be negotiated. This familiarity has the effect of minimizing both fatigue and anxiety associated with unfamiliar situations.

Foster co-supportive relationships

Above all it is important to have co supportive relationships with those who can offer guidance and strength in areas where you feel disadvantaged. It may be that you develop a special relationship with a non-alexithymic person, such as a friend, therapist, partner or workmate. The advantage here is that you can integrate your functioning with someone who can anchor you in emotional areas when and where you need it, someone who might gently steer you away from something when you are over-doing it to your detriment, or who can advise you on the emotional etiquette in various situations. In turn, you can help this person by supporting them in ways that you are skilled at giving, e.g. by offering them your neat reality sense and attention to details, giving a sports massage, by helping them with their mathematics homework or some other intellectual task, or with whatever other talents you have. But you should be forthright and tell the other that you cannot function proficiently in the emotional arena, and they are not to expect you to do so. This person should be encouraged to seek a measure of emotional fulfilment outside of your relationship, with others, which will help also to avoid a more problematic co-dependent style of relationship. A girlfriend/boyfriend would be a suitable partner for co-supportive activities because they are frequently present, or a second choice might be a friend, therapist or colleague (or indeed you may find several co-supportive relationships).

Take time out to gather your thoughts
Anecdotal evidence shows that those with alexithymia are able to process some emotional data but that it takes longer to do so because they use different parts of their brain to do this than others. Whereas a typical person might intuitively grasp emotional data in milliseconds, those with alexithymia experience a delay factor lasting anywhere from one extra second to several hours to arrive at the same conclusion. They have to think things out in a slower, rational manner, and to this aim 'time-out' rituals sometimes prove useful for catching on to the emotional values in situations and relationships.

Reflection time usually requires a private space free of distractions, such as a private bedroom, a study or locked bathroom, and is best practiced a few times each day. Other relatively distraction-free settings may be a meditation place, such as a church or ashram, a secluded nature spot, or while doing gentle sports like swimming, walking or gardening. The duration of time-out sessions is up to each individual, but it is best kept short so as to avoid practical reflection slipping into morbid rumination. Over-thinking about past slights, failed relationships, how difficult you find life, what people think of you, or where your life will end up in ten years leads only to morbidity and can bring on serious depression. It is therefore best to keep these reflective times focused on more practical emotional matters close at hand. A second recommendation is to terminate any time-out sessions in which only empty-headedness or confusion manifest, as nothing productive may take place at these times.

Overall, taking time out to gather your thoughts can improve your grasp of the feelings, intentions and expectations of others, as well as clarifying your own. This will greatly help your sense of clarity and ability to make informed decisions.

Family therapy

Most of the available writings about alexithymia treat it in isolation from the family context. Considering that alexithymic individuals live much of their lives within families, this leaves a gaping hole in our knowledge about how family relationships influence the alexithymic person, and about how it affects the wellbeing of non-alexithymic family members. One area which needs to be studied is the impact of attachment styles each member has with the alexithymic person, and vice-versa, and of whether these contribute to greater ease or disease in patterns of relating. For example, does a child's 'anxious attachment style' invite increased dependency behaviour by the alexithymic parent, and if so what issues does this impose on their interactions? Or if a partner or child has an 'avoidant attachment style', what are the characteristics of their interaction, and how best to negotiate the issues that arise? These are questions which can be explored in family systems therapy for the purpose of tailoring strategies and techniques to help family members cope on a healthier level.

Family therapy tends to view relationships in terms of the systems of interaction between family members and emphasizes family relationships as a key factor in psychological health. In this sense, family problems are seen to arise from a web of interactions within the family rather than being blamed on an individual member. The focus of therapy rests on how patterns of interaction maintain certain problems and assumes that the family unit is larger than the sum of its parts. While there is no data available for the benefits of family therapy for alexithymic and non-alexithymic family members, results from a variety of studies involving mentally ill and drug-addicted individuals and their patterns of relating with other family members reveals that family therapy is effective in raising awareness about the issues and alleviating some interactional stresses. There are typically between 5 and 20 sessions, in which a therapist usually meets all members of the family together. Some individual sessions may also be needed if an individual cannot communicate freely in the group setting. The proposition is that the patterns of relating in therapy mirror habitual interaction patterns at home, allowing interactional patterns in the session to become apparent both to the therapist and to the family for the further development of coping strategies.

For family therapy to be successful it is important for the therapist to have a working knowledge of alexithymia in order to properly assess its determining influence on communication patterns. It is not sufficient for the therapist to point out that the alexithymic individual is not listening to the feelings of others and that they should try harder. There must be an understanding of the deficits in emotional awareness, and any suggestions involving adjustment in communication must be based on this limitation.

As a further consideration, it is important to ask if children of the alexithymic parent are facing emotional crises requiring individual psychotherapy. If it is determined that the alexithymic environment is causing emotional damage, a child psychologist with knowledge about alexithymia may be able to help the child work though the experience of the emotionally unempathic relationship with the parent. A child who is still young may be more receptive to the experience of emotional attunement
provided by the therapist, enabling the gaining or regaining of emotional health.

Pharmacology

One use of combined pharmacological and psychotherapeutic intervention is to promote desired levels of affect regulation. When it comes to intense manifestations of affect the advantage of drugs is that they work rapidly in contrast to psychotherapeutic methods, although in the event of their discontinuation the disorders of dysregulated affect may quickly return. For this reason Taylor recommends the integration of pharmacologic and psychotherapeutic approaches in the context of treatment to help manage some disorders associated alexithymia (Taylor et al. 1997). Specifically, medications can be used to target anhedonia and depression (antidepressants), panic and anxiety (beta-blockers, anxiolytics, benzodiazepines), sleep disorders and tiredness (sedatives, soporifics), and mood instability (anticonvulsants, lithium). In helping to regulate the more distracting affective states these medications enhance the efficacy of bio- and imaginal-feedback techniques by allowing the individual to focus on the therapy instead of affective seizures.

Whilst bio- and imaginal-feedback have enormous potential to eliminate the need for long-term medication, there is of course the non-responsive case necessitating that pharmacological methods be maintained for long-term assistance.

Chapter 8

Assessment

How do I tell if I have alexithymia?

Below is a brief list of indicators which might suggest the presence of alexithymia. If you do have most or all of these traits and wish to pursue a formal diagnosis, the following sections detail clinical assessment questionnaires that you may be able to undertake upon request from a qualified clinician.

You may be alexithymic if:

- you find it hard to describe your emotions
- you are confused about the meaning of other people's emotional reactions
- you rely on principles to guide your behaviour rather than gut feelings
- you rarely fantasise about personal projects or wishes
- you sometimes have inexplicable bodily ailments
- other people find your speech long-winded or aimless
- other people find you somewhat pedantic
- other people find you unsentimental or lacking in feeling.

Beth Israel Questionnaire

The Beth Israel Questionnaire (BIQ) is one of the most widely used tools in the assessment of alexithymia. Developed by P.E.

Sifneos in 1973 to provide a systematic, standardized assessment of alexithymia, the tool consisted of 17 forced-choice questions that ask an interviewer to evaluate an individual's fantasy-life and emotional communication based on their responses. An additional six items consist of descriptions of the perceived therapeutic relationship. Within this 17-question collection Sifneos selected eight 'key' questions as markers of alexithymia, and only these answers are used in obtaining the alexithymia score. Due to criticisms of the BIQ method of gathering information, two additional requirements were added to improve its reliability – a broader range of responses to the questions were allowed, and all personnel asking the questions are trained in a standardized technique. More recently the BIQ was modified (Bagby, et.al. 1994) by eliminating nine of the questions which were not alexithymia-related, and adding in four new items which do target alexithymia. The result is a revamped 12-item BIQ consisting of six questions targeting emotional awareness, and six questions targeting imaginal activity and operative thinking. Initial testing of the 12-item modified BIQ has received positive results on its reliability (Taylor et al. 1997)

Toronto Alexithymia Scale

In 1985 Taylor and associates developed the Toronto Alexithymia Scale (TAS) consisting of 26 questions. This rating scale was the first reliable and valid self-report measure of alexithymia, which targeted four key factors:

1. eleven items on the ability to identify and describe feelings
2. seven items on the ability to communicate feelings
3. five items on the ability to daydream
4. six items on externally oriented thinking.

In 1992 the TAS was modified to incorporate updated knowledge about target factors. One of the changes worth noting here was the elimination of all questions directly assessing daydreaming and other imaginal activity which, short of being neglected, have been found to coincide with the presence or absence of other factor targets; that is, 'reduced imaginal processing' is apparently still being tapped by the revised questionnaire. The modified version was shortened from 26 to 20 questions, with a reduction from four to three target factors:

1. difficulty identifying feelings and distinguishing them from bodily sensations

2. difficulty describing feelings to others
3. externally oriented thinking.

Preliminary evidence of reliability and factorial validity has been well-established and the TAS-20 is now the most popular and widely used measure of alexithymia in the world, having been translated into Cantonese, Dutch, Finnish, French, German, Greek, Hebrew, Hindi, Italian, Japanese, Korean, Lithuanian, Polish, Portuguese, Spanish and Swedish (Taylor et al. 1997). In 2006 Bagby et.al published a 'Toronto Structured Interview for Alexithymia' (TSIA) which again included direct assessment of the imaginal processing which had been removed from the revised TAS-20.

Bermond-Vorst Alexithymia Questionnaire

The Bermond-Vorst alexithymia questionnaire (BVAQ) evolved from the Amsterdam 20-item questionnaire intended to assess five elements of alexithymia. Bermond and Vorst extended the questionnaire with the purpose of having two parallel versions, which led to the creation of the 40-item BVAQ. This questionnaire measures personality traits associated with experiencing, verbalizing, fantasizing, identifying and thinking about emotions, traits which are proposed to be essential for affect regulation. The BVAQ consists of five factor subscales:

1. emotionalising – the degree to which someone is emotionally aroused by emotion inducing events
2. fantasizing – the degree to which someone is inclined to fantasize, imagine, daydream etc.
3. identifying – the degree to which one is able to define one's arousal states
4. analysing – the degree to which one seeks out explanations of one's own emotional reactions
5. verbalizing – the degree to which one is able or inclined to describe or communicate about one's own emotional reactions.

The BVAQ includes a reliable measure of reduced fantasy life, whereas two successive revisions of the Toronto Alexithymia Scale have discarded all the items directly assessing daydreaming and other imaginal activity. The Bermond-Vorst questionnaire has been through several successful validation trials and is also gaining fast popularity as a reliable alternative to the TAS-20 (Bermond and Vorst 2001).

Alexithymia Questionnaire for Children

Whilst alexithymia is a trait assumed to be present in some children, it has scarcely been looked at apart from one Japanese study where a rudimentary questionnaire was designed for assessment by school teachers (Fukunishi, Yoshida & Wogan 1998).

Recently a self-report measure named the Alexithymia Questionnaire for Children was constructed based on the original TAS-20 and re-written in simpler language. The questionnaire consists of three target factors to which the 20 questions are aimed:

1. seven items for difficulty identifying feelings
2. five items for difficulty describing feelings
3. eight items for externally oriented thinking.

Initial studies have confirmed that the core features of the adult alexithymia questionnaire could be identified in children with reliability using the modified scale (Rieffe, Oosterveld & Terwogt 2006).

Considering the pre-operational imagination-bound modes of cognitive functioning in children, one might question the continuing absence of items which target constricted imaginal processes, as evidenced by a paucity of fantasies. This is a rich ground for assessment in the young whose use of symbolic fantasy is inconsistent with adult modes of formal operational thought and functioning. That children may be more amenable to questions on the nature of their fantasies and 'play activities' suggests a potential area of development for the current questionnaire.

Online Alexithymia Questionnaire – G2

The Online Alexithymia Questionnaire (OAQ) was developed by this author in 2005 in response to perceived shortcomings of the previous alexithymia questionnaires such as the Bermond-Vorst or TAS-20. Three problems presented: the poorly targeted questions regarding constricted imaginal processes; the confusion experienced by the alexithymic subject when asked to recognize if they do, or don't, experience the normal range of feelings; and the unavailability of testing instruments to the general public.

The first of these perceived shortcomings concerns the very nature of imagining, which needed elaboration before questions could be economically targeted to the deficit in question. Discussions with alexithymic individuals revealed that many believed their imaginal capacity was intact, leading to positive questionnaire responses regarding their ability to daydream, imagine or fantasise. With the introduction of Edward Casey's (1976) distinction between the controlledness and spontaneity in a given act of imagining, it became evident that commentaries regarding the absence of alexithymic imagining were referring to a deficit in 'spontaneous' or 'unconscious' imagining, and not to controlled imagining. With this knowledge the OAQ questions were written to reflect this distinction. For example: 'I use my imagination mainly for practical means, eg., like how to work out a problem or construct a useful idea or object' and 'My imagination is usually not spontaneous and surprising, but rather used/employed in a more controlled fashion' or, inversely scored, 'My imagination is often spontaneous, unpredictable and involuntary.'

The second shortcoming related to the older wording of questions targeting difficulty identifying feelings and difficulty describing feelings. Whilst these factors are integral features of the alexithymia construct, the very nature of these deficits in the alexithymic individual may obscure recognition of their relative presence or absence as requested by the questionnaires. With this in mind we sought to alter or delete some of the overly direct questions. For example, e.g. questions like 'I don't know why I feel angry' were not repeated, and wordings such as 'I have feelings that I can't properly identify' were replaced with a less assured 'I can't identify feelings that I vaguely sense are going on inside of me'. We also included a further set of questions asking what 'other people say' about the alexithymic individual's emotional communication, and reduced the number of items which presume an introspective ability of the individual to be aware of their deficits in emotional communication. For example, we added 'People tell me I don't listen to their feelings properly, when in fact I'm doing my utmost to understand what they are saying!' or 'I don't like people's constant assumptions that I should understand or guess their needs… it's as if they want me to read their minds!' and 'People tell me to describe my feelings more, as if I haven't elaborated enough'.

Third, we wanted to create an accessible free guide for general practitioners and lay public for the purpose of gaining amateur assessment which might indicate the need for more thoroughgoing clinical assessment. At the moment recognized alexithymia questionnaires are expensive and difficult to acquire without clinical degrees in relevant disciplines, and it is hoped that the OAQ might fill the gap.

Further features of the OAQ include two subcategories; 'Vicarious interpretation of feelings' and 'Sexual difficulties and disinterest', which target interpersonal behaviours co-extensive with traits of alexithymia. Of the second of these, extensive discussions with alexithymic adults revealed common experiences of difficulties with sexual relations and activities, with descriptions of disturbing bodily sensations (associated with affect) and personal confusion regarding the sexual expectations and feelings of others. Although the individual's sexual libido may be functioning on a healthy level, the 'pseudophobia' (Krystal 1988) surrounding the emotional component of sexual intimacy is manifest as a reluctance to indulge in sexual act, or as a preference for sexual encounters involving low emotional intensity.

In May 2007 the Online Alexithymia Questionnaire underwent a revision of nine questions that had similarities to wordings in the Toronto Alexithymia Scale (TAS-20), with duplications being replaced by more original phrasing. The resultant changes to the OAQ have created a second-generation questionnaire (G2) reflecting its ongoing evolution as independent from other alexithymia measures. The Online Alexithymia Questionnaire – G2 consists of 37 questions divided among the following factor targets:

F1 DIFFICULTY IDENTIFYING FEELINGS

F2 DIFFICULTY DESCRIBING FEELINGS
F2-B VICARIOUS INTERPRETATION OF FEELINGS
F3 EXTERNALLY ORIENTED THINKING
F4 RESTRICTED IMAGINATIVE PROCESSES
F5 PROBLEMATIC INTERPERSONAL RELATIONSHIPS
F5-B SEXUAL DIFFICULTIES AND DISINTEREST

BarOn Emotional Quotient Inventory

Based on 19 years of research by Dr Reuven BarOn and tested on
over 120,000 individuals worldwide, the BarOn Emotional Quotient
Inventory (EQ-i) is designed to measure a number of constructs
related to emotional intelligence (BarOn 2004). This instrument is
the first scientifically validated self-report measure for emotional
intelligence, and assesses one's ability to deal with daily
environmental demands and pressures. The EQ-i consists of 133
items composed of 15 subscales: emotional self-aware- ness,
assertiveness, self-regard, self-actualisation, independence, empathy,
interpersonal relationship, social responsibility, problem solving,
flexibility, reality testing, stress tolerance, impulse control,
optimism, and happiness. A youth version of the adult questionnaire
has also been constructed for children aged 7 to 18 yrs (BarOn EQ-
i:YV) (BarOn and Parker 2000).

Parker, Taylor and Bagby (2001) examined the relationship between
the alexithymia construct and emotional intelligence, as measured by
the TAS-20 and EQ-i, in a group of 734 adults. Results revealed that
the constructs overlap and are inversely related, indicating that those
scoring in the higher range on various alexithymia scales are likely
to score in the low range on emotional intelligence measures.

Scored Archetypal Test

The Scored Archetypal Test (SAT-9) represents a significant
complement to other measurements in assessing imaginal, fantasy
and symbolic functioning in alexithymia (Cohen, Demers-Desrosiers
& Catchlove 1983). This test was adapted from Gilbert Durand's
theory of the structures of imagination (Durand 1999, first published
1960) and works by tapping an individual's ability to form 'possible

scenarios' in imagination. The test works by presenting an individual with nine symbolic images – a sword, a fall, an animal, water, something with cyclical characteristics, a refuge, a devouring monster, a character, and fire – who is then asked to draw a picture linking these images in one, and also to write a story with the same objective. If the degree of alexithymia of the subject is in the high range, the drawings and stories lose their subtlety and originality (one might hypothesize due to the absence of the spontaneous trait factor of imagining). When the symbolic function is impaired, the individual cannot use symbols to create a myth, betraying the individual's inability freely to symbolise 'what may be' in their daily life and relationships.

The SAT-9 demonstrates projective imaginal techniques reliably, and with further investigation of precisely which traits of imagining constitute the impairment in alexithymia, the measure may be refined to reflect findings and complement questionnaires that presently do not target imaginal deficits.

Two-Factor Imagination Scale (TFIS)

The Two-Factor Imagination Scale is a self-report measure developed in 2008 to assess spontaneous imaginal activity. Although useful for assessing any individual, the TFIS was created for assessing imaginal activity in high alexithymic individuals who by definition evidence "constricted imaginal processes, as evidenced by a paucity of fantasies" (Taylor, Bagby & Parker 1997, p.29). The constricted imaginal processes of alexithymia refer to a lack of spontaneous imagining (Thompson, 2008, 2009), and to affect laden imagery in particular (Aleman, 2005). The deficit in spontaneous or unconscious imagining is also elaborated by prior researchers Fain and David (1963), McDougall (1985), and Krystal (1988).

To understand spontaneous imagining it is helpful to contrast it with the activity of controlled imagining. The factor structure of the TFIS is based on American philosopher Edward Casey's descriptions of controlled and spontaneous imagining which he terms "traits of imagining" (1976, p.63) Casey describes controlled imagining as a willful effort to manipulate images in the mind which is characterized by three sub-traits: 1. initiation, 2. guidance, and 3.

termination, whereas spontaneous imagining is described as self-generating and is characterized by the subtraits 1. effortlessness, 2. surprise, and 3. instantaneity. Casey demonstrates that although the traits of spontaneous and controlled imagining tend to compliment each other they are nevertheless exclusive, meaning that when we imagine it will be either spontaneous or controlled in character in a given moment and cannot be both "at the same time," although in practice the two acts of imagining often appear in close proximity and can give rise to each other in a symbiotic interplay. (Casey, 1976; 1991)

The TFIS cut-off scores were determined after an informal assessment of 4 high-alexithymic and 4 low-alexithymic individuals. The first group had previously undertaken a TAS-20 assessment with a qualified clinician within the previous two years and scored in the high-alexithymia range 61+, with subsequent scores on the TFIS being 38, 42, 39, and 34. From this result the first cut-off score of equal to or less than 45 for 'low spontaneous imagination' was selected. The second group selected randomly from the local Queensland community each completed the informal Online Alexithymia Questionnaire-G2 and all scored in the low-alexithymia range 94-, with subsequent scores on the TFIS being 62, 55, 61, and 53. From the results of this second (low-alexithymia) group the cut-off point for 'high spontaneous imagination' was set at equal to or greater than 60, and 'proportionate spontaneous/controlled imagining' was set at 46 to 59. This preliminary survey does not constitute a formal study and further clinical investigations will be required to validate the selected thresholds. Nevertheless, initial indications suggest that the TFIS may have potential for detecting the 'constricted imagination' factor of alexithymia.

Although the TFIS rates spontaneous imagining with a higher score, this should not be assumed to indicate a value judgment of psychological health. Whilst psychological health is usually characterized by a high degree of spontaneous imagination (Winnicott, 1971), there are notable exceptions to this rule in which a florid imagination can portend psychological disorder such as may be found in delusional, or schizoid states for example. Conversely, whilst a high degree of controlled imagining may be correlated with psychological disorders involving intellectualisation, there are exceptions where, for example, one's culture, profession or current life circumstances require a stronger emphasis on controlled imagining. Finally, the TFIS is provided for gaining informal assessment which may indicate the need for a more thoroughgoing clinical assessment, or to compliment existing alexithymia measures. A TFIS score does not represent a diagnosis.

-TFIS FACTOR TARGETS-

Factor 1: Spontaneous Imagining

(a) Effortlessness

· My imagination persistently generates daydreams and fantasies without any conscious effort on my part.
· When designing or inventing something, or when participating in artistic activities, my imagination often directs the process with little mental deliberation.
· When a friend feels upset my imagination automatically generates an internal image of their predicament, helping me to understand what they are feeling.
· (inverse) The products of my imagination take considerable effort to construct.

(b) Surprise

· My daydreams and fantasies frequently produce unexpected themes.
· I am frequently astonished at the scenarios my imagination generates.
· My imagination tends to conjure/suggest realities contrary to those I would habitually expect.
· (inverse) The products of my imagination are generally predictable.

(c) Instantaneity

· Elaborate imaginary themes often come to me instantaneously, seemingly out of nowhere.
· My imagination produces elaborate scenarios in an instant without prior deliberation on the theme.

· (inverse) The images and scenarios of my imagination usually take time and persistence to construct.

Factor 2: Controlled Imagining

(a) Initiation

· The products of my imagination are usually ones that I initiate; i.e. they generally don't come on their own.
· Imagining is an act I choose to commence; it is rarely something that just "happens to me".
· I use my imagination mainly for practical means, eg., like how to work out a problem or construct a useful idea or object.
· (inverse) I frequently find myself imagining something, even when I have not chosen to do so!

(b) Guidance

· My imagination is usually not spontaneous and surprising, but rather is used/employed in a more controlled fashion.
· I tend to guide the direction of my imaginative processes, rather than relying on the possibility that imagination will autonomously guide the process.
· When I imagine something I prefer to control the contents, direction, spatial character, and duration of the imagined scenario.
· (inverse) I often do not have control, nor take control of an imaginative experience, but allow the contents, direction and spatial characteristics of the imaginal presentation to direct themselves.

(c) Termination

· I tend to terminate imaginal exercises once I have reached a pre-determined or desired goal of the activity.
· I usually terminate impractical or unwanted imaginal exercises by distracting myself, emptying my mind, or by initiating a brand new exercise in imagination.
· (inverse) I tend to allow imaginative experiences to reach their own natural conclusion, rather than me calling a halt to the activity.

This Two-Factor Imagination Scale is a first generation questionnaire which may be updated if future studies indicate areas for improvement, in which case 'G-2' (etc.) will be applied. The Two-Factor Imagination Scale is copyrighted (c)-2008 and may be used by individuals without permission, or reproduced in professional settings or for study/research purposes for free with permission from the author.

Chapter 9

An Exploration of Alexithymia and Metaphor

Have you felt so proud to get at the meaning of poems? Stop this day and night with me and you shall possess the origin of all poems. - Walt Whitman

With these words Whitman announces that his audience will possess the creative origins and meaning of poems if they stop with him awhile. Little was he aware that some individuals suffer a profound inability to identify creative metaphor, an inability which would in turn render some in his audience unable to appreciate the *poesis* of his poems.

Alexithymia affects about one in ten people and is characterized by (a) an inability to generate spontaneous metaphors nor readily understand metaphors in a non-literal sense, and (b) an inability to identify emotions in self or others. Rather than apprehending his world by means of imagination, the alexithymic person relies on 'a stimulus bound, externally oriented cognitive style' (Taylor, G.J *et.al* 1997) which consists in a concrete sense-interpretation of metaphor akin to Jung's description of the extraverted sensing style:

No other human type can equal the extraverted sensation type in realism. His sense for objective facts is extraordinarily developed. His life is an accumulation of actual experiences of concrete objects, and the more pronounced his type, the less use does he make of his experience. In certain cases the events in his life hardly deserve the name "experience" at all. What he experiences serves at most as a guide to fresh sensations; anything new that comes within his range of interest is acquired by way of sensation and has to serve its ends (Jung, C.G. 1971, p. 52).

The alexithymic individual may appreciate the structural aspects of poetry such as rhyming, juxtaposition, meter, and geometric layout, but he finds it difficult to spontaneously appreciate its metaphorical nuances other than in conventional ways or as literal statements. The explanation underneath the following poem by Whitman 'Shut Not Your Doors' shows a literalist interpretation by an alexithymic man who was asked what this poem suggested to him:

Shut not your doors to me proud libraries,
Because that which was lacking on all your well-fill'd shelves, yet needed most, I bring,
Forth from the War emerging, a book I have made,
The words of my book nothing, the drift of it every thing,
A book separate, not link'd with the rest nor felt by the intellect,
But you ye untold latencies will thrill to every page

To the first line *Shut not your doors to me proud libraries/* this individual suggested: "Ok that means the author is willing to go to the library?" The literal interpretation here suggests that he did not see the metaphorical implication of library as a place of bounded knowledge, a place which may be enhanced by an openness to unforeseen knowledge. Clearly Whitman would not have been satisfied that this man had "possessed the meaning" of his poem, and it is doubtful that he would have learned poetry's meaning even had he sat at the master's feet through an entire recitation of *Song of Myself*. The concrete alexithymic imagination cannot free the image from it's sensory aspect as it makes no attempt to *deform* the images, and as Gaston Bachelard reminds "If there is no change, or unexpected fusion of images, there is no imagination.... There is only perception, a memory of perception, a familiar memory, an habitual way of viewing form and colour." (Bachelard, G. 1988)

There are some cases in which alexithymic individuals learn to understand metaphors in the sense of a *sign* with a numerically limited value where, for instance, a fire is a sign of anger (and anger only), or a heart a sign of love (and love only) or a cross is the sign of Jesus' Crucifixion (and Jesus' Crucifixion only). The metaphor is not allowed to suggest itself with multiple random possibilities and is forced to comply with the pre-packaged, prior-learned definition. The individual may develop a repertoire of fixed metaphorical signs as a basis from which to interpret poetic images, but signs which more often appear meaningless in contexts where the poem's intended meanings depart from the sign's locked-in definition. Here (in the use of signs) metaphor becomes a literalistic exercise of a mind searching for definitional certainty. Noesis in place of poesis. Such sign language functions for the alexithymic individual as an intellectual compensation for his deficit in spontaneous imagination, reminding of how a colour-blind individual must make intellectual compensations for his deficit in colour detection.

For such persons the phrase *poetry blindness* is apt as referring to the inability to 'see' the limitless possibilities and ambiguity presented by the poetic image. The alexithymic individual sees limited possibilities in a poetic image which renders the metaphor unable to "suggest itself" as an ambiguous and limitless pool of potential. Or said more accurately the metaphorical image *does* suggest itself, but to a person who has little sense by which to receive it, ie. little spontaneous imagination. George Lakoff and Mark Johnson suggest, in their book 'Metaphors To Live By,' that there are two very different understandings of metaphor. The first they term *conventional metaphors* which have agreed and standardized meanings that help structure the conceptual system of our culture, and the second are metaphors that are outside our standardized conceptual system which they term *imaginative* or *creative metaphors* which pose new realities rather than a preexisting ones. Therefore it is the inability to envisage the latter which characterizes alexithymic perception and sets these individuals at a handicap when trying to appreciate the potential implications of a metaphor or poem.

In the face of this anomaly the question arises of what or who is blocking the ability to imagine spontaneously? According to psychoanalysis the culprit is the mechanism of *primal repression*, a theoretical blocking impulse which, unlike in normal repression (where imaginal contents do crystallize in awareness but are subsequently banished) does not allow for spontaneous images to form at the outset, meaning there are no hidden images to uncover through therapy.... the images simply have not formed. To translate this deficit into the language of archetypal psychology we might say there is a *lacuna*, i.e. in this case a complete absence of creative imagining. In an attempt to describe such lacuna James Hillman writes, "Something is fundamentally missing. Your character, your personality inventory has a hole in it. Your crimes are not due so much to the *presence* of shadow, but rather to a specific absence, the lack of human feeling [and] other traits may fill out the absence: impulsiveness (the short fuse), shortsightedness, repetitive rigidities, emotional poverty." (Hillman, J. 1996 p.234). Furthermore, we cannot be tricky and imagine that the individual has "a lacuna way of seeing" or that he sees "by means of lacuna", for this smacks of a projection to quiet our own fear of the imagination-less state. The alexithymic individual does not see by means of lacuna, rather, he simply does not see.

In the spirit of archetypal psychology we might locate a mythical person in the act of primal repression, a figure who personifies the image-blocking agency. Here I propose as culprit Apollo the God of intellect and conceptual clarity, the one to whom Whitman was perhaps appealing to *shut not his doors*, ie. to the one who might be persuaded to *unblock* his proud enclave of knowledge and accept spontaneous untold latencies which await. Aside from his splendid portrayals as god of art and science, Apollo has a negative aspect as an intellectual tyrant who tries to bind all Cassandrian revelations to himself, or otherwise render them unintelligible to those who might hear. As suggested by James Hillman: "Apollo certainly presents a pattern that is disastrous, destructive for psychological life, cut off from everything that has to do with feminine ways, whether Cassandra or Creusa or Daphne -whomever he touches goes wrong- so that you have the feeling that Apollo simply doesn't belong where there is psyche." (Hillman, J. 1983 p.25).

Because alexithymic individuals tend to fare poorly in personal and interpersonal life, a sympathetic nerve is struck in therapists who want to cure those afflicted or at least make an improvement in functioning. Therapy of alexithymia is a growing industry, with therapists of every ilk making grand claims of their ability to shift the alexithymic blockage of imagination: art, poetry, play, dance, archetypalist, Jungian, psycho-dynamic, cognitive, relational and other therapies each vie for the claim of 'best alexithymia therapy', but what few are willing to do is see the phenomenon of alexithymia as it is, phenomenologically, without reference to either aetiology or well-meaning proscriptions for improvement. Therapists attempt to evoke responses through art, play, poetry, and symbolic narratives and are frequently successful in evoking physical emotional arousal in the individual, but such bodily-reactions still leave the aroused person utterly clueless as to how to *imagine* the emotions which have been unleashed in his body. For the full circle of emotional processing to be completed a further extrusion of our emotions is required "through yet another interpretive grid- now applied not to the situation the emotion is about but to the emotion itself as a state of the subject" (Roberts. R.C. 2008). This suggests that the *evoking* image (via art images, etc.) is not enough to break through the alexithymic armor, and that it takes a further act of *representing the emotion in image form* to complete the circle of awareness and hence to "make soul". But it is not even certain that the alexithymic individual has the capacity to creatively imagine his emotional arousal, such is the reality and steadfastness of his lacuna.

Evoking emotion via skillful exposure to imaginal stimuli brings us no closer to what is required for the alexithymic individual to represent his emotional arousal in imagination, to find emotion's face, and in most cases if the individual is coaxed to paint, sing, write poetry, or dance, he is doing so according to a controlled mental process and pre determined concepts which may 'seem' to represent his emotional arousal but which on closer examination is lacking true creativity. Evoking emotion in the absence of spontaneous imagining proves pointless to this group of people, people who may already be swamped with emotional excitation but cannot frame and contain the excitation within creative secondary images. Here we come to a dead end, a situation described well by Rafael Lopez-Pedraza who writes

'with these patients the motto I have [usually] adopted – "The image, what makes possible the impossible"- simply does not work. To 'make possible' is to 'make conscious' an image that has been 'impossible'. These patients, however, are unable to form an image; or just when one thinks an image is in process, something coming from nowhere destroys any such possibility. Sometimes, one can see

that when they offer what could be called an image, there are no accompanying psychical feelings or creativity. What one is taking as an image which could move the psyche is, for them, a stereotype, a mimetism.' (Lopez-Pedraza, R. 1990)

To summarize, there are some people who despite their ardent desire to understand the metaphorical possibilities in poetry, are often unable. Perhaps imagination is something that alexithymic persons cannot trust (Plaut, F. 1966), or perhaps they find the image too terrifying to face (Micklem, N. 1979), but phenomenologically speaking we can say they have a severe lacuna in place of spontaneous imaginal ability which, as Guggenbuhl-Craig and Hillman insist, is the best way to honour the presented fact: i.e. there is no childhood aetiology and no fantasized cure toward which we strive, just the emptied imagination and blank face betraying that nothing has arisen. The alexithymic person simply doesn't "get" creative metaphor and tends by way of compensation to employ cogitation in place of imagination:

Mr. Cogito and the Imagination

*Mr. Cogito never trusted
tricks of the imagination*

*the piano at the top of the Alps
played false concerts for him*

*he didn't appreciate labyrinths
the Sphinx filled him with loathing*

*he lived in a house with no basement
without mirrors of dialectics*

*jungles of tangled images
were not his home*

*he would rarely soar
on the wings of metaphor
and then he fell like Icarus
into the embrace of the Great Mother*

he adored tautologies
explanations
idem per idem

that a bird is a bird
slavery means slavery
a knife is a knife
death remains death

he loved
the flat horizon
a straight line
the gravity of the earth

        -Zbigniew Herbert

Whitman's desire to have all comers participate in the creative act of poesis is an ambitious one which may fall shy of the mark for some listeners, but this very failure of imagination serves as a reminder that we might count ourselves among the fortunate to get at the meaning of poems.

Chapter 10

Emotional intelligence is really *imaginal* intelligence

"For when an emotion is not held aesthetically within its images… Then emotion runs rampant and we have to damp it down with drugs or exorcise it through therapies of release and expression. Instead, I am suggesting that restoration of the imagination is the fundamental cure of disordered emotion". (Hillman, 1960)

Alexithymia, a Greek term meaning literally 'without words for feelings' designates the inability to identify and describe one's own, or others' emotional states, and is synonymous with the concept of low emotional intelligence (Parker, Taylor & Bagby 2001). The purpose of this study is to highlight the stunted imagination characteristic of this condition, and to speak for its restoration by appeal to the storytelling wise-guy Silenus.

Before exploring the role of imagination in alexithymia I need to clarify two words: *emotion* and *feeling*, which in everyday language tend to be used interchangeably. Below I use these terms in their more strict psychiatric sense where emotion refers to physical arousal evidenced by such signs as smiling, crying, laughing, body tension, blushing, tight stomach, posturing, voice intonation, rapid breathing, elevated pulse etc., and where feeling refers to one's mental recognition and understanding of manifestations of emotional arousal. Alexithymic individuals may display full-blown bodily emotions, but they are unable to identify these emotions nor understand their significance on a mental level. To put it another way, alexithymia involves an essential deficit in one's ability to evaluate feelings, but not in the realm of emotional excitation which can often be present in *excess*.

Clinically alexithymia is defined by the following four factors:

> (i) difficulty identifying feelings and distinguishing between feelings and the bodily sensations of emotional arousal
> (ii) difficulty describing feelings to other people
> (iii) constricted imaginal processes, as evidenced by a paucity of fantasies; and
> (iv) a stimulus-bound, externally oriented cognitive style
> (Taylor, Bagby and Parker 1997, p.29)

The constricted imaginal processes of alexithymia refer to a lack of spontaneous imagining (Thompson, 2008, 2009), and to affect laden images in particular (Aleman, 2005), a lack posing enormous disadvantages for personal and interpersonal functioning when one considers that imagination is a meaning maker *par-excellence* in all human experience. In agreement with James Hillman (1983), we can say that spontaneous fantasy images are 'primary psychological data' which present a mental image of physiological arousal; data which provides the necessary material for concluding and articulating specific feeling states. Stated alternatively by Antonio Damasio, an individual senses "a feeling" arising from the activation of emotion, "provided the resulting collection of neural patterns becomes images in the mind." (1999, p.79)

Lacking these imaginal signifiers the alexithymic individual is left searching for the meaning of his emotional excitation in the face of numerous environmental and physiological stimuli. To give a hypothetical example:

Paul is driving to a party with his girlfriend and notices his heart is racing, and so asks himself, "Is my heart racing because I'm angry at the driver who just cut in front of me without using his indicator? Is my heart racing because I'm anxious about being in a crowded room of strangers at the party? Is my heart racing because I'm in love with my girlfriend and my heart is all a-flutter? Is my heart racing because I'm excited about the music and dancing that we are about to enjoy? Or is my heart racing because I forgot to take my blood-pressure medication before going out? (Etc.).

In this scenario there are five distinct possibilities, and it may prove impossible to tell which is the stimulus responsible for his racing heart based on bodily signals or environmental clues alone. In this situation the popular therapeutic proscriptions for biofeedback tend to prove ineffective because the signals being fed back from Paul's emotional body provide insufficient detail to allow a conclusive evaluation from the five equally plausible explanations. Paul simply cannot identify which emotion is responsible for his elevated heart-beat: anger, anxiety, love, excitement, or indeed high blood-pressure.

The precision of imaginal feedback on the other hand shows the specific face of emotion where (to continue with the above example) Paul's rapid heart beat appears in conjunction with a spontaneously generated image of the other driver cutting in front of him without indicating and Paul –still in imagination- blasting his horn at the offending driver. The sudden inrush of the fantasy image allows him to identify therefore that the beating is of an 'angry heart'. This is an example of autonomous psyche in its self-generative glory.

Cultivation of imaginal feedback consists in deliberate contemplation of spontaneously produced images with the aim of enriching conscious understanding of somatic arousal. Fantasy images can help one identify emotions as they happen, as in the above example of becoming aware of one's beating heart (biofeedback) but being faced with five competing explanations regarding the emotion involved. In that instance the internal fantasy image of a careless driver cutting in without using his indicator provided Paul with the necessary data with which to identify the emotion being experienced. By accessing imaginal signifiers the absent emotional understanding can be unlocked for the alexithymic individual, allowing for verbal articulation and intelligent modulation of emotional states. This proposition finds agreement in the words of alexithymia expert Graeme Taylor who writes:

> '...techniques that promote imaginal activity are likely
> to strengthen referential links between symbolic and
> subsymbolic elements within a patient's emotional

schemas (Bucci 2002). Increasing referential activity renders the patient more aware of feelings and therefore better able to reflect on and regulate states of emotional arousal.' (Taylor & Taylor-Allan 2007, p.218)

Archetypal Psychology, as elaborated by James Hillman (1983) provides a sophisticated set of guidelines for evoking, and vivifying imagination in the therapeutic setting, a process having immediate value for enriching the impoverished imagination of alexithymic individuals. This method asks the therapist to be guided by questions such as; "How well has the image worked? Does the image release and refine further imagining? Does the therapist's response 'stick to the image' as the task at hand, rather than associate or amplify into non-imagistic symbolisms, personal opinions, and interpretations?" (Hillman 1983, p.21). To these questions we can add another; 'How well has the patient's image worked to help identify an emotion?' The therapist and patient must use these questions to guard against losing the nascent image through intellectual distractions.

These guidelines hold the therapist to the task of 'animating the image', because according to the premises of archetypal psychology the image is the primary psychological datum, in which feelings are as complex as the image that contains them (Hillman 1983). This approach necessitates that therapy "return personal feelings (anxiety, desire, confusion, boredom, misery) to the specific images which hold them. Therapy attempts to individualize the face of each emotion: the body of desire, the face of fear, the situation of despair. Feelings are imagined into their details. This move is similar to the imagist theory of poetry (Hulme 1924), where any emotion not differentiated by a specific image is inchoate, common, and dumb..." (Hillman 1983, p.59).

If we look to mythological language we might say that the emotional god Dionysus *needs* his tutor Silenus in order to make sense of the emotions at play or be left otherwise to suffer meaningless emotional eruptions within his body. Silenus teaches Dionysus the value of ecstasy, of how to name and frame a life of emotion without being torn to pieces by the unmodulated intensity of passion. In his volume on Dionysus Rafael Lopez-Pedraza concurs, 'We can speculate that, without being tutored, a Dionysiac nature would remain "wild" and "mad" and unable to connect to any immediate sense of reality..... Silenus offers an archetypal image for a psychotherapist who can constellate and "teach" a Dionysiac psychology, one who can "read" and "differentiate" emotions.' (Lopez-Pedraza 2000, p.35)

Silenus is characterised as a wise teacher in the Symposium where Alcibiades suggests both he and Socrates look similar in their physical attributes and both contain images of fascinating beauty "on the inside". The latter reference is to popular ancient statuettes of Silenus which opened at the front to show his insides full of small golden figurines of the gods, an internal richness which both he and Socrates are said to possess as teachers. What might the internal richness of Silenus' teaching be? In the story of his encounter with King Midas we are given a leading clue;

> 'One day, the debauched old satyr Silenus, Dionysus former pedagogue, happened to straggle from the main body of the riotous Dionysian army as it marched out of Thrace into Boeotia, and was found sleeping off his drunken fit in the rose gardens. The gardeners bound him with garlands of flowers and led him before Midas, to whom he told wonderful tales... Midas, enchanted by Silenus's fictions, entertained him for five days and nights, and then ordered a guide to escort him to Dionysus's headquarters. Dionysus, who had been anxious on Silenus's account, sent to ask how Midas wished to be rewarded.' (Graves, 1992, p.281)

Silenus's teaching comes as creative storytelling and it is this that he offers Midas and others who seek his wisdom. He sings his stories, says Virgil, to a throng of revellers who dance in tune to the beat, stories not of feasting or jolly drunkenness but of pathos; Prometheus' guilty theft, the mariner's sad cries for a lost Hylas, Pasipae's morbid desire for the white bull, the unrequited loves for Atalanta, Scylla terrifying trembling sailors, and the bitter revenge of Philomena against abusive Tereus. (Virgil, Eclogue IV). The benefit of such stories for bringing insight to the emotional excitations of the *dionysia* is invaluable, and for this it is no surprise to find Dionysus and his tutor portrayed as inseparable co-revellers. Indeed Silenus appears in iconography as a janus face with Dionysus, suggesting two faces of a single *emotional process archetype*. This is akin to Jung's notion of an affect-image continuum by which he characterised archetypal images as portraits of emotions that allow the emotion to consciously "perceive itself" (Jung, CW 8). Using Jung's metaphor of a spectrum of light to describe this process, where the infra-red end represents physical emotional arousal and the ultra-violet end represents psychic imagery, we might say that Dionysus and Silenus are the infra-red and ultra-violet of each emotional act.

Apollo, with whom Dionysus is often associated in the thinking of psychologists and philosophers, presents an antithesis: he holds a rational point of view which Lopez-Pedraza reminds is outside the body and therefore outside Dionysus's archetypal boundaries (Lopez-Pedraza, 2000). On this basis it is little wonder Nietzsche went insane trying to reconcile the irreconcilable; emotion and intellect push apart like two poles of a magnet, or at least do not communicate in a shared language. Silenus and Dionysus on the contrary are one in their shared 'irrationality'.

Without his other face Dionysus is vulnerable to dangers posed by the Titans and by Apollo, with the former goading to violent emotional excess and the latter to intellectual repression of emotional fantasy. Perhaps Apollo's repressive influence works in favour of the Titanic excess by nullifying all emotion-containing imagination -binding Silenus- so the Titans can have their way?

Recommendations that may drive the alexithymic individual "mad" include naïve proscriptions for 'expressing your emotions' such as by therapies of dance, song, art, drama or primal-screaming. Without spontaneous Silenean imagination the emotions evoked can reach manic pitch in which the arts serve as Titanic invitations that push the individual beyond his ability to cope. While it is true these mediums evoke or provoke emotional arousal within a limiting setting and therefore may be useful for people who already possess a degree of emotional awareness, the *alexithymic* individual tends to become confused, overwhelmed, distressed, anxious or traumatized by the excessive emotions released (which may already be present in maddening degree prior to the experiment). The individual may become humiliated by being subjected to an outside person's experiment which has succeeded in little more than provoking an embarrassing excess of emotions without providing any new skills for identifying or modulating their intensity. The problem with such rituals is that they come from outside, the images are not generated within the individual psyche from whom the emotion is being extracted. Therein lies the proscription for how to conduct these practices with the person who has a deficit in emotional awareness; at some point in the process he needs to generate his own scenarios to dance to, or at least creatively distort those images given to him in order to consciously participate. We need those little golden images to appear from the inside to guide the process, and not be introduced or artificially planted from without. Soul cannot be made by an injection of strychnine.

Finally, the awakening of imaginal feedback can benefit by suggestions from Henry Krystal which take into account the alexithymic individual's pseudophobia surrounding self-control of emotional life, and in particular of the use of imagination to this end. These are "powers" writes Krystal, "reserved for mother, doctor, God"... but most certainly not for oneself (1988 p.317). Before the work of accessing imagination can proceed, the therapist must relieve this pseudophobia so that the individual feels he has "permission" to allow spontaneous imagination and to make use of it in identifying and regulating emotion expression. Krystal writes, "Eventually, the benign mental representations become so secure that the direct use of a security blanket can be given up. Dreams, fantasy, and play can be used... so that self-caring can be carried out" (1988 p.335)

In summary, for the full circle of *emotional process* to take place imagination needs to reflect not just the scenario that provoked the emotion but also elaborate the emotion itself as a state of the subject. As in the example of 'Paul' above who is moved to anger by the image of a careless driver, imagination extrudes a further image of himself blasting a horn at the offending driver, effectively 'putting himself in the picture'. This is identical to nocturnal dreams in which 'I' am portrayed in the dream and am behaving in a certain way in response to the situation presented. Only in this way is it possible to complete the circle of awareness and hence "make soul". The boon is portrayed on an ancient Porto sarcophagus (see Miller, 1981) which depicts our storytelling Silenus offering a young male initiate a butterfly, the Greek word for which is "soul".

Afterword

A note on classification

Many descriptors and classifications have been proposed for
alexithymia, among them being; condition, disorder, syndrome,
thinking style, state, trait, illness, emotional dysregulation, cognitive
distortion, neurotic defence, temperament, neural anomaly, fantasy
configuration, difference, disease, and more. These may be grouped
into informal descriptors, erroneous descriptors, and formal
classifications.

Alexithymia is a syndrome which in psychiatric language refers to
a cluster of symptoms occurring together which indicate a particular
psychological abnormality. It may also be called a condition which
refers more generally (and vaguely) to an individual's state of being.
As a syndrome alexithymia includes a bundle of characteristics
including operative thinking, emotional dysregulation, lack of
spontaneous imagination, anhedonia, external orientation, and
difficulty identifying and describing feelings. It is inappropriate to
use the terms neurotic defence, temperament, thinking style, neural
anomaly, physical disease or illness as hypotheses are either
incorrect or yet to be proven.

Formal classifications proposed for alexithymia include state,
personality trait, or disorder. Arguments for construing secondary
alexithymia as a state cite the transitory nature of the condition as
secondary to panic, anxiety, depressive, posttraumatic and other
conditions in which the alexithymia disappears when the stressors
are removed or symptoms alleviated. Primary alexithymia on the
other hand is an enduring personality trait, that changes little over
time or with changing circumstances. The majority of patient follow-
up studies reveal that alexithymia is a stable personality trait, though
there are notable exceptions of state alexithymia suggesting that
alexithymia may not be reliably viewed as either a state or trait. Use

of these terms in individual cases, then, may be best dictated by history taking and follow-up studies.

Although alexithymia is a clinically defined concept it does not at present constitute a diagnostic illness apart from other conditions it may accompany. As it has not been officially classified and listed in DSM and ICD manuals it is controversial to describe it as a disorder, though there is a building case for its consideration as an independent cognitive-affective disorder.

Lastly, referring to an alexithymic individual's differences rather than to deficits, disorders or defects of personality is gaining some currency in common parlance. Whilst there is still a valid place for citing specific deficits involved in alexithymic emotional processing, the reference to differences will have the benefit of reducing unnecessarily disparaging attitudes towards people with alexithymia.

Appendix A

Two-Factor Imagination Scale

1. My imagination persistently generates daydreams and fantasies without any conscious effort on my part.
More often true | Less often true

2. My daydreams and fantasies frequently produce unexpected themes.
More often true | Less often true

3. Elaborate imaginary themes often come to me instantaneously, seemingly out of nowhere.
More often true | Less often true

4. The products of my imagination are usually ones that I initiate; i.e. they generally don't come on their own.
More often true | Less often true

5. My imagination is usually not spontaneous and surprising, but rather is used/employed in a more controlled fashion.
More often true | Less often true

6. I tend to terminate imaginal exercises once I have reached a pre-determined or desired goal of the activity.
More often true | Less often true

7. When designing or inventing something, or when participating in artistic activities, my imagination often directs the process with little mental deliberation.
More often true | Less often true

8. I am frequently astonished at the scenarios my imagination generates.
More often true | Less often true

9. My imagination produces elaborate scenarios in an instant without prior deliberation on the theme.
More often true | Less often true

10. Imagining is an act I choose to commence; it is rarely something that just "happens to me".
More often true | Less often true

11. I tend to guide the direction of my imaginative processes, rather than relying on the possibility that imagination will autonomously guide the process.
More often true | Less often true

12. I usually terminate impractical or unwanted imaginal exercises by distracting myself, emptying my mind, or by initiating a brand new exercise in imagination.
More often true | Less often true

13. When a friend feels upset my imagination automatically generates an internal image of their predicament, helping me to understand what they are feeling.
More often true | Less often true

14. My imagination tends to conjure/suggest realities contrary to those I would habitually expect.
More often true | Less often true

15. The images and scenarios of my imagination usually take time and persistence to construct.
More often true | Less often true

16. I use my imagination mainly for practical means, eg., like how to work out a problem or construct a useful idea or object.
More often true | Less often true

17. When I imagine something I prefer to control the contents, direction, spatial character, and duration of the imagined scenario.
More often true | Less often true

18. I tend to allow imaginative experiences to reach their own natural conclusion, rather than me calling a halt to the activity.
More often true | Less often true

19. The products of my imagination take considerable effort to construct.
More often true | Less often true

20. The products of my imagination are generally predictable.
More often true | Less often true

21. I frequently find myself imagining something, even when I have not chosen to do so!
More often true | Less often true

22. I often do not have control, nor take control of an imaginative experience, but allow the contents, direction and spatial characteristics of the imaginal presentation to direct themselves.
More often true | Less often true

Scoring for questions:

For questions 1, 2, 3, 7, 8, 9, 13, 14, 18, 21, 22, add 3-points per question if you answered "More Often True" and 1-point for each answer of "Less Often True".

For questions 4, 5, 6, 10, 11, 12, 15, 16, 17, 19, 20, add 1-point per question if you answered "More Often True" and 3-points for each answer of "Less Often True".

Forcing a respondent to give an answer to each question may cause frustration because it is quite possible that a particular question just doesn't apply, thus disrupting the flow of the process. For this reason, unanswered questions are defaulted as "undecided" and given a medium score of 2-points.

Maximum possible score is 66. This test uses cutoff scoring: equal to or less than 45 = low spontaneous imagination, equal to or greater than 60 = high spontaneous imagination. Scores of 46 to 59 = proportionate spontaneous/controlled imagining.

References

Aleman, A. (2005) Feelings you can't imagine: towards a cognitive neuroscience of alexithymia, Trends in Cognitive Sciences, Volume 9, Issue 12 , Pages 553-555

Attwood, T. (2006) The Complete Guide to Asperger's Syndrome. London: Jessica Kingsley Publishers.

Attwood, T. and Gray, C. (1999) Discovery Criteria. Accessed on 20
December 2006 at www.as-if.org.uk/criteria.htm

Bach, M., Bach, D., Bohmer, F. and Nutzinger, D.O. (1994a) 'Alexithymia and somatization: Relationship to DSM-III-R diagnoses.' Journal of Psychosomatic Research 38, 529–538.

Bach, M., de Zwaan, M., Ackard, D., Nutzinger, D.O. and Mitchell, J.E. (1994b) 'Alexithymia: Relationship to personality disorders.' Comprehensive Psychiatry 35, 239–243.

Bachelard, Gaston. (1988) Air and Dreams: An Essay On the Imagination of Movement. The Dallas Institute Publications.

Bagby, M., Taylor, G.J., Parker, J.D.A, Dickens, S.E., (2006), The Development of the Toronto Structured Interview For Alexithymia: Item Selection, Factor Structure, Reliability and Concurrent Validity, Psychotherapy and Psychosomatics, 75: 25-39.

Bagby, M., Taylor, G.J., Parker, J.D.A.: (1994) The twenty-item Toronto Alexithymia Scale -- II. Convergent, discriminant, and concurrent validity. Journal of Psychosomatic Research, 38: 33-40,

BarOn, R. (2004) 'The BarOn Emotional Quotient Inventory (EQ-i): Rationale, description, and summary of psychometric properties.' In G. Geher (ed) Measuring Emotional Intelligence: Common Ground and Controversy. Hauppauge, NY: Nova Science Publishers.

BarOn, R. and Parker, J.D.A (2000) BarOn Emotional Quotient Inventory: Youth Version (EQ-i:YV): Technical Manual. Toronto: Multi-Health Systems.

Baron-Cohen, S., Joliffe, T., Mortimore, C. and Robertson, M. (1997) 'Another advanced test of theory of mind: Evidence from very high functioning adults with autism or Asperger syndrome.' Journal of Child Psychology and Psychiatry 38, 813–822.

Bazydlo, R., Lumley, M.A. and Roehrs, T. (2001) 'Alexithymia and polysomnographic measures of sleep in healthy adults.' Psychosomatic Medicine 63, 56•61.

Bermond, B. and Vorst, H.C. (2001) 'Validity and reliability of the Bermond-Vorst Alexithymia Questionnaire.' Personality and Individual Differences 30, 413–434.

Berthoz, S. and Hill, E.L. (2005) 'The validity of using self-reports to assess emotion regulation abilities in adults with autism spectrum disorder.' European Psychiatry 20, 3, 291–298.

Bruch, H. (1962) 'Perceptual and conceptual disturbances in anorexia nervosa.' Psychosomatic Medicine 24, 187–194.

Casey. E.S. (1976) Imagining: A Phenomenological Study (Studies in Continental Thought). Bloomington, IN: Indiana University Press.

Casey, E.S (1991) Spirit and Soul; Essays in Philosophical Psychology. Spring Pub.

Cochrane, C.E., Brewerton, T.D., Wilson, D.B. and Hodges, E.L. (1993) 'Alexithymia in eating disorders.' International Journal of Eating Disorders 14, 219–222.

Cohen, K.R., Demers-Desrosiers, L.A. and Catchlove, R.F.H (1983)
'The SAT-9: A qualitative scoring system for the AT-9 test as a measure of symbolic function central to alexithymic presentation.' Psychotherapy and Psychosomatics 39, 77–88.

Damasio. A. (1999) The Feeling of What Happens, Harcourt and Brace

Durand, G. (1999) The Anthropological Structures of the Imaginary. Trans. by Margaret Sankey and Judith Hatten. Brisbane: Boombana Publications.

Fain, M., & David, C. (1963) 'Aspects fonctionels da la vie onirique. Revue Francaise de Psychoanalysis 27, 241-243

Fitzgerald, M and Molyneux, G. (2004) 'The overlap between alexithymia and Asperger's syndrome.' Letter to the Editor; American Journal of Psychiatry 161, 2134–2135.

Freud, S. (1925) 'Negation' 1925 International. Journal of Psycho-Analysis., 6 (4), 367-71.

Fukunishi, I., Yoshida, H. and Wogan, J. (1998) 'Development of the alexithymia scale for children: A preliminary study.' Psychological Reports 82, 43–49.

Graves, R. (1992) The Greek Myths, complete edition. Penguin.

Goleman, D. (1996) Emotional Intelligence: Why It Can Matter More Than IQ. London: Bloomsbury Publishing.

Grotstein, J.S. (1986) 'The borderline as a disorder of self regulation.' In J.S. Grotstein, M.F. Solomon and J.A. Lang, (eds) The Borderline Patient: Emerging Concepts in Diagnosis, Psychodynamics, and Treatment. Hillsdale, NJ: The Analytic Press.

Haviland, M.G., Hendryx, M.S., Shaw, D.G. and Henry, J.P. (1994) 'Alexithymia in women and men hospitalised for psychoactive substance dependence.' Comprehensive Psychiatry 35, 124–128.

Haviland, M.G., Sonne, J.L. and Kowert, P.A. (2004) 'Alexithymia and psychopathy: Comparison and application of California Q-set prototypes.' Journal of Personality Assessment 82, 306–316.

Hill, E., Berthoz, S. and Frith, U. (2004) 'Brief report: Cognitive processing of own emotions in individuals with autistic spectrum disorder and in their relatives.' Journal of Autism and Developmental Disorders 34, 2, 229–235.

Hillman, J. (1983) Archetypal Psychology: A Brief Account. Putnam, CT: Spring Publications.

Hillman, J. (1983) Inter-Views. Spring Publications.

Hillman, J. (1996) The Soul's Code: In Search of Character and Calling. Random House Inc..

Honkalampi, K., Hintikka, J., Laukkanen, E., Lehtonen, J. and Viinamäki, H. (2001) 'Alexithymia and depression: A prospective study of patients with major depressive disorder.' Journal of Psychosomatics 42, 229–234.

Hoppe, K.D. and Bogen, J.E. (1977) 'Alexithymia in twelve commissurotomized patients.' Journal of Psychotherapy and Psychosomatics 28, 148–155.

Horgan, T.G. and Smith, J.L. (2006) 'Interpersonal reasons for interpersonal perceptions: Gender-incongruent purpose goals and nonverbal judgment accuracy.' Journal of Nonverbal Behavior 30, 3, 127–140.

Joukamaa, M., Saarijarvis, S. Muuriaisniemi, L. and Salokangas, R.K.R. (2006) 'Alexithymia in a normal elderly population.' Comprehensive Psychiatry 37, 144–147.

Jung, C.G. (1967) Alchemical Studies. Volume 13 of the Collected Works of C.G. Jung. Bollingen Series XX. Princeton, NJ: Princeton University Press.

Jung, C.G. (1971) Psychological Types. Volume 6 of the Collected Works of C.G. Jung. Bollingen Series XX. Princeton, NJ: Princeton University Press.

Jung, C. G., (1969) The Structure and Dynamics of The Psyche, CW-6, Bollingen, Princeton University Press. [Note: Although Jung refers in this volume to an archetype-instinct continuum, in his *Definitions* in CW 6 he makes clear that emotions are equally considered instinctive actions. See *instinct* on p.451]

Kashdan, T.B., Elhai, J.D. and Frueh, B.C. (2006) 'Anhedonia and emotional numbing in combat veterans with PTSD.' Behaviour Research and Therapy 44, 3, 457–467.

Keltikangas-Jarvinen, L. (1990) 'Alexithymia and type A behaviour compared in psychodynamic terms of personality.' British Journal of Medical Psychology 63, 131–135.

Krystal, H. (1968) Massive Psychic Trauma. New York: International Universities Press.

Krystal, H. (1988) Integration and Self-Healing: Affect, Trauma, Alexithymia. Hillsdale NJ: The Analytic Press.

Lakoff, G., and Johnson, M., (1980) Metaphors We Live By. University of Chicago Press.

Langs, R.J. (1978) 'Some communicative properties of the bipersonal field.' International Journal of Psychoanalytic Psychotherapy 7, 87–135.

Levant, R. (1997) 'Men and emotions: A psychoeducational approach.' From The Assessment and Treatment of Psychological Disorders Video Series. New York: Newbridge Communications.

Levant, R.F. and Pollack, W.S., (1995) A New Psychology of Men. Basic Books, Harpur Collins

Litz, B.T., Orsillo, S.M., Kaloupek, D. and Weathers, F. (2000) 'Emotional processing in posttraumatic stress disorder.' Journal of Abnormal Psychology 109, 1, 26–39.

Lopez-Pedraza, R. (1990) Cultural Anxiety. Daimon Verlag, Switzerland.

Lopez-Pedraza, R. (2000) Dionysus in Exile: On the Repression of the Body and Emotion, Chiron Publications.

Marty, P. and de M'Uzan, M. (1963) 'La pensée opératoire.' Revue Française de Psychoanalyse 27, 1163–1177

Masterson, J.F and Klein, R. (1995) Disorders of the Self: New Therapeutic Horizons. New York: Brunner/Mazel.

McDougall, J. (1985) Theaters of the Mind: Illusion and Truth on the
Psychoanalytic Stage. New York: Basic Books.

McDougall, J. (1989) Theaters of The Body: A Psychoanalytic Approach to Psychosomatic Illness, Norton

Micklem, N. (1979) The Intolerable image: The Mythic Background of Psychosis. Spring Publications

Miller, D. (1981) Christs: Meditations on Archetypal Images of Christ. The Seabury Press.

Moriguchi, Y., Decety, J., Ohnishi, T., Maeda, M., Mori, T., Nemoto, K., Matsuda, H. and Komaki, G. (2007) 'Empathy and judging other's pain: An fMRI study of alexithymia.' Cerebral Cortex 17(9): 2223 - 2234

Nemiah, C.J. Freyberger, H. and Sifneos, P.E. (1976) 'Alexithymia: A View of the Psychosomatic Process.' In O.W. Hill (1970) (ed)

Modern Trends in Psychosomatic Medicine, Vol 2. London: Butterworths.

Nemiah, C.J. and Sifneos, P.E. (1970) 'Affect and fantasy in patients with psychosomatic disorders.' In O.W. Hill (ed) Modern Trends in Psychosomatic Medicine. Vol 2. London: Butterworths.

Nemiah, J.C., Sifneos, P.E. and Apfel-Savits, R. (1977) 'A comparison of the oxygen consumption of normal and alexithymic subjects in response to affect provoking thoughts.' Psychotherapy and Psychosomatics 28, 167–171.

Parker, J.D.A., Taylor, G.J. and Bagby, R.M. (2001) 'The relationship between emotional intelligence and alexithymia.' Personality and Individual Differences 30, 107–115.

Plaut, F (1966) Reflections on Not Being able to Imagine. in Analytical Psychology: A Modern Science, ed. Fordham, M. et al, Heinemann, London (1973).

Posse, M., Hallstrom, T. and Backenroth-Ohsako, G. (2002) 'Alexithymia, social support, psycho-social stress and mental health in a female population.' Nordic Journal of Psychiatry 56, 5, 329–334.

Rieffe, C., Oosterveld, P. and Terwogt, M.M. (2006) 'An alexithymia questionnaire for children: Factorial and concurrent validation results.' Personality and Individual Differences 40,123–133.

Roberts. R.C. (2008) in Corrigan, J. The Oxford Handbook of Religion and Emotion. Oxford Uni.. Press.

Rybakowski, J., Zasadzka, M., Zasadzka, T. and Brzezinski, R. (1988) 'High prevalence of alexithymia in male patients with alcohol dependence.' Drug and Alcohol Dependence 21, 133–136.

Salminen, J. K., Saarijarvi, S., Aarela, E., Toikka, T., Kauhanen, J., (1999) Prevalence of alexithymia and its association with sociodemographic variables in the general population of Finland Journal of psychosomatic researchVol 46, pp.75-82

Sifneos, P.E. (1973) 'The prevalence of "alexithymic" characteristics in psychosomatic patients.' Psychotherapy and Psychosomatics 22, 255–262.

Sondergaard, H.P. and Theorell, T. (2004) 'Alexithymia, emotions and PTSD: Findings from a longitudinal study of refugees.' Nordic Journal of Psychiatry 58, 3, 185–191.

Taylor, G.J., Bagby, R.M. and Parker, J.D.A. (1997) Disorders of Affect Regulation: Alexithymia in Medical and Psychiatric Illness. Cambridge: Cambridge University Press

Taylor, G.J., Parker, J.D.A. and Bagby, R.M. (1990) 'A preliminary investigation of alexithymia in men with psychoactive substance dependence.' American Journal of Psychiatry 147, 1228–1230.

Taylor, G.J., & Taylor-Allan, H.L. (2007) Applying emotional intelligence in understanding and treating physical and psychological disorders: What have we learned from alexithymia, Chapter 15 in-Educating People to be Emotionally Intelligent, by Eds. Reuven Bar-On, Kobus Maree, J. G. Maree, Maurice J. Elias. Praeger (2007)

Thompson, J. (Aug. 2008) Alexithymia: An Imaginative Approach, Psychotherapy in Australia Journal, Volume 14, No 4, Pages 58-63

Virgil: Eclogues, Georgics, Aeneid. Translated by Fairclough, H. R., Loeb Classical Library, Volumes 63 & 64. Harvard University Press, (1916).

Wastell, C.A. and Taylor, A.J. (2002) 'Alexithymic mentalising: theory of mind and social adaptation.' Social Behavior and Personality 30, 141–148.

Weiner, H. and Fawzy, F. (1989) 'An integrative model of health, disease, and illness.' In S. Cheren (ed.) Psychosomatic Medicine: Theory, Physiology and Practice 1, 9–44.

Whitman, W. (1977) The Complete Poems. Penguin.

Winnicott, D.W. (1940) 'Ego distortion in terms of true and false self.' In D.W. Winnicott (1965) The Maturational Process and the Facilitating Environment. Madison, CN: International Universities Press.

Winnicott, D.W. (1949) 'Mind and its relation to the psyche-soma.' In D.W. Winnicott (1958) Through Paediatrics to Psycho-Analysis. New York: Brunner/Mazel.

Winnicott, D.W., (1971) Playing and Reality. Tavistock Publications

Zeitlin, S.B. and McNally, R.J. (1993) 'Alexithymia and anxiety sensitivity in panic disorder and obsessive-compulsive disorder.' American Journal of Psychiatry 150, 658–660.

Reading Material

To date there are few books published on the subject of alexithymia, though with increasing interest new titles may come into circulation in the near future. Apart from scattered journal articles one may attempt to collect, below are a few published titles on the subjects of alexithymia, emotion and imagination.

Alexithymia

Disorders of Affect Regulation: Alexithymia in Medical and Psychiatric Illness (1997) by Graeme J. Taylor, R. Michael Bagby and James D.A. Parker, Published by Cambridge University Press, Cambridge.

Integration and Self-Healing: Affect, Trauma, Alexithymia (1993) by
Henry Krystal (ed) The Analytic Press, Hillsdale, NJ.

Theaters of the Mind: Illusion and Truth on the Psychoanalytic Stage (1991) by Joyce McDougall, published by Routledge, London.

Alexithymia among Orthodox Jews: The Role of Object Relations, Family Environment, and the Presence of a Disabled Sibling (2006) by ProQuest/UMI.

Toward a Theory of Psychosomatic Disorders: Alexithymia, Pensée Opératoire, Psychosomatisches Phanomen (1977) by Walter Brautigam, published by S. Karger AG.

Alexithymia: A Psychological Analysis Based on Clinical and Healthy Individuals (2001) by Modjtaba S. Mortazavi Asl, published by Uppsala University.

Alexithymia: An Imaginative Approach, (2008) by Jason Thompson; Psychotherapy Australia Journal, vol 14, No 4, Aug.

Emotion and feeling

Disorders of Affect Regulation: Alexithymia in Medical and Psychiatric Illness (1997) by Graeme J. Taylor, R. Michael Bagby and James D.A. Parker, published by Cambridge University Press, Cambridge.

The Handbook of Emotional Intelligence: Theory, Development, Assessment, and Application at Home, School and in the Workplace (2000) by Reuven Bar-On and James D.A. Parker (eds), published by Jossey-Bass, San Francisco.

Emotional Intelligence: Why It Can Matter More Than IQ (1996) by Daniel Goleman, published by Bloomsbury, London.

Emotion: A Comprehensive Phenomenology of Theories and their Meanings for Therapy (1997) by James Hillman, published by Northwestern University Press, Evanston, IL.

Inferior Feeling and Negative Feeling' in Jung's Typology (1986) by Marie-Louise von Franz and James Hillman, published by Spring Publications, Dallas.

Education of the Feeling Function' in Jung's Typology (1986) by Marie-Louise von Franz and James Hillman, published by Spring Publications, Dallas.

Descartes' Error: Emotion, Reason, and the Human Brain (1994) by Antonio R. Damasio, published by Grosset/Putnam, New York.

The Feeling of What Happens: Body and Emotion in the Making of Consciousness (1999) by Antonio R. Damasio, published by Harcourt Brace, New York.

Emotion Regulation in Couples and Families (2006) by Douglas K. Snyder, Jeffrey A. Simpson, and Jan N. Hughes, published by American Psychological Association, Washington DC.

Emotional Intelligence in Everyday Life (2006) by JosephCiarrochi, Joseph P. Forgas, and John D. Mayer, published by Psychology Press, New York and Hove

Stoicism and Emotion (2007) by Margaret R. Graver, published by The University of Chicago Press, Chicago and London

The Oxford Handbook of Religion and Emotion, by John Corrigan, published by Oxford University Press, New York

Religion and Emotion: Approaches and Interpretations (2004) by John Corrigan, published by Oxford University Press, New York

Faithful Feelings: Rethinking Emotion in the New Testament (2006) by Mathew A. Elliott, published by Kregal Publishing, Grand Rapids

Imagination

Imagination and Its Pathologies (2003) by James Phillips and James Morley, published by MIT Press, Cambridge, MA.

Archetypal Psychology: A Brief Account (Uniform Edition, Vol. 1) (2004) by James Hillman, published by Spring Publications, Putnam, CT.
Re-Visioning Psychology (1992) by James Hillman, published by HarperCollins, London.

Dream and the Underworld (1979) by James Hillman, published by Harper and Row, New York.

Healing Fiction (1983) by James Hillman, published by Spring Publications, Putnam, CT.

Working with Images (2000) by Benjamin Sells (ed), published by Spring Publications, Putnam, CT.

Imagining: A Phenomenological Study (Studies in Continental Thought) (2000) by Edward S. Casey, published by Indiana University Press, Bloomington, IN.

Spirit and Soul: Essays in Philosophical Psychology (2004) by Edward S.
Casey, published by Spring Publications, Putnam, CT.

The Anthropological Structures of the Imaginary (1999) by Gilbert Durand, translated by Margaret Sankey and Judith Hatten, published by Boombana Publications, Brisbane.

Poetics of Imagining: From Husserl to Lyotard (1991) by Richard Kearney, published by HarperCollins, London.

The Wake of Imagination: Toward a Postmodern Culture (1988) by Richard Kearney, published by University of Minnesota Press, Minneapolis, MN.

An Approach to the Dream', and Defense and Telos in Dreams' in Echo's Subtle Body (1992) by Patricia Berry, published by Spring Publications. Putnam, CT.

Waking Dreams (1994) by Mary Watkins, published by Spring Publications, Putnam, CT.

Invisible Guests: The Development of Imaginal Dialogues (1990) by Mary
Watkins, published by Sigo Press, Boston, MA.

Force of Imagination: The Sense of the Elemental (2000) by Paul Sallis, published by Indiana University Press, Bloomington, IN.
Symbolization and Desymbolization: Essays in Honour of Norbert Freedman (2002) Edited by Richard Lasky, published by Karnak, New York

Metaphors We Live By (1980) by George Lakoff and Mark Johnson, published by University of Chicago Press, Chicago, IL.

Imagination Is Reality: Western Nirvana in Jung, Hillman, Barfield, and Cassirer (1979) by Robert Avens, published by Spring Publications, Putnam, CT.

Playing and Reality (1991) by Donald W. Winnicott, published by Routledge, London.

www.ingramcontent.com/pod-product-compliance
Lightning Source LLC
Chambersburg PA
CBHW050459290526
45786CB00006B/2358